ROBES OF LIGHT

The Nine Egyptian Light Bodies embodied in Modern Experience

ACKNOWLEDGEMENTS

I give thanks to innumerable people who have gifted me with their presence, among them: Roe Adams, Allegra Alquist, Robert Aiken, Omraam Mikael Aivanov, Carolyn Anderson Sherry Anderson, Joel and Serfina Andrews, Jose Arguelles, Angeles Arrien, Fritjof Bergmann, William and Joan Beuhler, Bojalina Boatman, Brook Medicine Eagle, John Broomfield, Sally Burdick, Eileen Caddy, Peter Caddy, Joseph Cambell, Dominie Cappadona, Nicolas Carter, Geoffrey Chandler, Paul Check, Nicole Christine, Sister Mirium Clare, Dale Clark, Barbara and Jerry Clow, Joseph Mark Cohen, Cathy Coleman, Craig Comstock, Flora Courtois, Sheryl Cotleur, Roger Davis, Constance Demby, David Doolittle, Sophia Douglas, Rocco and Mary D'Ordine, Gayle Dulcy, Frank Sanje Elliott, George Feuerstein, Anthea Francine, Maxine Freed, John Gibbon, Eric Gladwin, Jonathan Glazier, Marilyn Goggin, Jonathan Goldman, Goenka, John Gross, Steve and Deborah Haines, Steven Halpern, Noora Hansen, Irina Harfold, Suzanne Harrill, Kelly and Rosanna Hart, John Haugse, Clare Heartsong, Elgin and Doris Heinz, Ruth-Inge Heinze, Barbara Hero, Tamara Hill, Ana Holub, Don Hunter, Marty Immerman, Julian Isaacs, Morgan Johnson, Bill Kautz, Donald Keyes, Jai Klarl, Jonathan Klimo, Michael Korba, Stanley Krippner, Charles Leary, John Wayne Lee, Richard Leviton, Richard Lucas, Karl Maret, John Maschino, Avon Mattison, Mitchell May, Terrance McKenna, Ralph Metzner, Zenon Michalak, Harold Moses, Simeon and Maia Nartoomid, Will Nofke, Ted Odza, Anita Rui Olds, Omraya, Lawrence Ostrow, Neera and Pan Paine, John Perry, Barbara Pettee, Charles Ponce, Jull Purse, Marcia Noren, John and Joann Reeves, Pennel Rock, Alma Rose, Vern Rutsala, Lee Sanella, Touson Saryon, Will and Kalima Sawyer, Lawrence Schechter, Rupert Sheldrake, John Shultz, William Stafford, Taki Stanicci, Ron Starwolf, Nancy and Richard Stoddart, David Surrenda, Shunryu Suzuki Roshi, Willow Trujillo, Sir George Trevelyn, Barbara and Lee Van Cleef, Diana Vandenberg, Marcel Vogel, Leslie Walker, Eunice Watson, Mary Carol Weber, Jack Wilkinson, Berney Williams, Fred Alan Wolf, Jack and Patty Wright, Jim Yandell, Jeff Volk, Arthur and Ruth Young, Gary Zucav.

note from the author: When I was in the second grade, I capitalized Nature and Art, and was always corrected by the teacher with red marks. I continue to capitalize these words.

This book is dedicated to all beings who are sincere in their life processes, enabling true initiations more and more into the Light and Supreme Source

The images and suggestions given in this book on the three spiritual bodies are to be taken in quietly and deeply into the most subtle aspects of yourself. Each character has different colors, symbols, patterns—which are all light-codes. Although there is a universal myth, there are individual variations, different ways of transforming passion into compassion.
What this means is changing only self-interest to the good of the whole. This means quietly and humbly serving: people, plants, animals, and beings of higher dimensions.

Printed in Hong Kong

All original illustations and book design by Rowena Pattee Kryder

FIRST EDITION, published by Golden Point Productions, Crestone, CO 81131

Library of Congress Control Number: 2005924140   isbn 0-9722747-3-1

ROBES OF LIGHT

The Nine Egyptian Light Bodies embodied in Modern Experience

by Rowena Pattee Kryder, Ph.D.

Golden Point Productions
Crestone, Colorado

Foreword

Rowena Pattee Kryder's *Robes of Light: The Nine Egyptian Light Bodies embodied in Modern Experience* is a brilliant expression and demonstration of A Divine Human Being's co-creative accomplishment in sincerely living one's process with full awareness and intention.

As a full expression of joy, *Robes of Light* successfully speaks to Divine Human Being In Love with Prime Source. Through the gifts of clarity, continuity and process this master culture creator intentionally embraces compassionate relationships with divine love, divine self, divine beings and divine creation in microcosmic and macrocosmic levels.

This is a remarkable book of instruction and guidance on, *How to embrace and be embraced by our life process with grace, awareness and intention.*

Visual illustrations and words of art speak to the whole being by invoking and evoking questions and emotions of the heart-mind. This profound gift encompasses the full spectrum of Divine Human Initiations as revealed through the process of formation. We are blessed with informational guideposts of clarity and form through extensive understanding and relationship with harmonics, color, sacred geometry, cosmic nature beings and universal accompaniment.

In gratitude and blessing, I honor Rowena for her dedication of continually providing usable methods which speak to the certainty of the balanced being. This mindful experiential process of formation is a cosmic breakthrough which provides the individual with enlightened tools to measure, shape and form personal foundation and understanding as the whole being seeks awareness of personal truth.

As you move through the processes and encounter the initiations, revelations of self awareness and beauty will embrace you and you will know your self in your fullest intention of being who you really are.

Willow Tequillo, Native America/Asian Medicine Woman

ROBES OF LIGHT—CONTENTS

Part One: Light Bodies

Part Two: Robes of Light

Part One
LIGHT BODIES

In numerous traditions—Egyptian, Taoist, Greek, Islamic, Jewish, Christian, Shaivite, Hindu, African, Polynesian, Amerindian, Theosophical—there is an awareness of the subtle bodies, sometimes called light bodies, that reside within and emanate from human beings. This is because, not only human beings, but all beings, have light codes within them. What are light codes? They are pure eternal light information that is behind and within even the genetic code. Light codes are a gift from Prime Source, containing the symbols and archetypes—pure information—that enables a being to be what it is.

Light codes do not contradict evolution, but rather evolution is a complement to light-codes. For evolution takes the light codes and incorporates them into energy, connection, and substance so that beings become manifest. Without evolution there would be no display or manifestation of the codes or patterns of Prime Source.

If you have been conditioned to believe to the contrary, you may drop this book at once, or read on, for you may find out something useful for your own evolution.

In the first chapter I will give a brief synopsis of an Egyptian understanding of light bodies which also goes along with consciousness and understanding of the human role in the cosmos. Later we will explore archetypes.

To understand what we are, as humans, I have found researching and practising the sacred texts of different cultures resonant with the essence of my being. We know that what is changing—impermanent—cannot be who we are. Not only our physical bodies change, but our emotions and thoughts, even our aspirations and will change. I deeply know that there is something immortal in us that is eternally present, even if it eludes our perceptions, feelings, and thoughts. Many years ago, in the sixties, with intense kundalini experiences, these kinds of questions led me to study sacred texts of various cultures. The questions I asked were:

1) Where did we come from and where are we going?
2) Is there a purpose to our lives and the universe, and if so, what?
3) If there is a purpose it must be built into us. What, then is the fundamental structure and function of our being?

These questions boil down to the nature of our energy bodies or light bodies, and how we live our lives—in consciousness, word, and action.

In the first part of this book the Egyptian Nine Light Bodies are presented as a basis for the light body unfoldment of the stories of twenty four characters and archetypes.

In the second part, you will find many exercises, in color and pattern, sacred geometry and harmonics, that can help you know what archetypes you resonate most to. Then there are nine Initiations. Our twenty-four characters each goes through these initiations in various ways. And as they do so, they find resonance with more and more archetypes, moving more and more towards their soul purpose. It is intended that the reader recognize which archetypes and psychic attractors they resonate to most.

Being honest with oneself and wanting the truth about oneself are the main prerequisites. The characters all have "shadows" (Khaibit in Egyptian) that need to be faced and acknowledged. The conscience (Ab) sees one through this difficult passage and then the soul (Ba) is more revealed.

The three spiritual "bodies" are presented last. The characters have already integrated various archetypes, moving toward integration of self, and surrender to the Oneness.

Chapter One: THE EGYPTIAN NINE LIGHT BODIES

In the Egyptian *Book of the Dead* (*The Book of Going Forth By Day*) nine bodies are delineated in the context of the text. Although there are various interpretations of what these bodies mean, in the following I have given some suggestions, based on my own experience, originally inspired by Maia Christine's work, http://www.spiritmythos.org/

The Ren is the power of the name as a signature of resonance to a person. There are words of power and each consonant and vowel has an archetypal quality. Finding one's Ren is like finding one's genetic code. It is a cosmic signature within us, and it relates to our physical vehicle. The Egyptians used the Ren in such a way that by calling one's name is to have power over one.

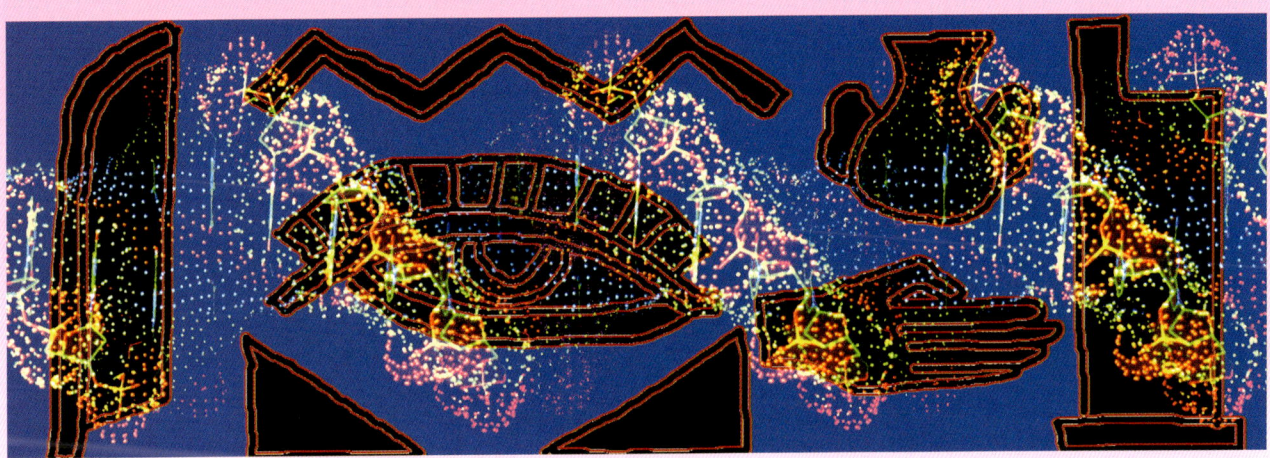

The REN holds a personal signature

When you discover your spiritual name, you have the power to be in greater alignment with your soul, for the Ren is the spiritual name that Prime Source gives you, and that sustains through all life-times.

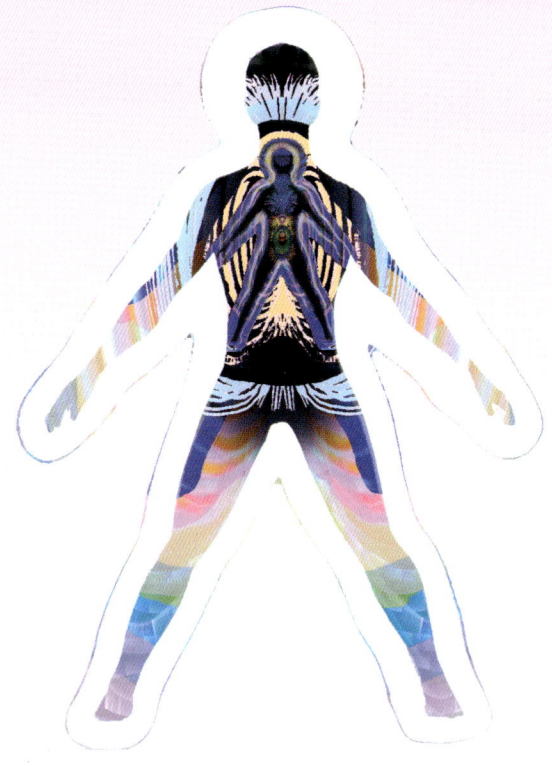

The KHAT is a template for the physical vehicle, perhaps like a hologram, a pattern that holds matter in its resonant place as organs and bodily systems. The KHAT is a directive code for the physical.

The KHAT is a hologram

The KA is the etheric double and subconscious

The Ka is the etheric double, but it also holds a self-image through a subconscious latency, which by itself, may be very limiting. Its aim is to define the physical body, give it energy and form, but also the Ka has desires of its own. It could be said to be the subconscious and body image.

The Ka has a sort of imagination, within limits, that influences the body image through subconscious fears and desires. The Khat duplicates what the Ka imagines and then the physical body responds to desires and fears with addiction or balance, gaining or losing weight, or any number of physical ailments or achievements.

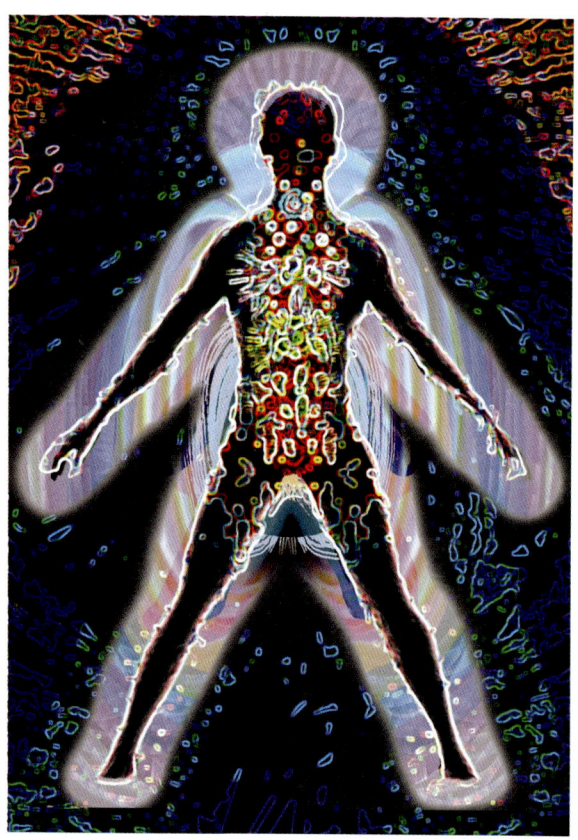

The KHAIBIT

The Khaibit is the rectifier of emotions and thoughts. It is the shadow, which has a life of its own in terms of its mythic reality. The Khaibit is a realm of polarity, for the shadows are cast from another reality above it. All the physical bodies are in the realm of polarity as well, for they are "deposits" of the psycho mental bodies (Khaibit and Ab). The Khaibit could be said to be our shape-shifting unconscious where our mythic realities are played out, unknown to our consciousness. The myth lived by the Khaibit affects the life of the Ka. Making conscious the unconscious of the Khaibit is essential if a personal myth is to be revealed. To find one's mythic reality is not the same as finding one's soul purpose. It is, rather, to know the Khaibit's relation to the Ka, Khat, and Ren as an integration, and to be receptive to inspiration from "above" (spiritual bodies). The myths of the world contain the mysteries of the Khaibit's life for a humanity composed of innumerable races. The Egyptian story of Horus and Set is a battle of higher and lower selves becoming whole (Osiris-Isis).

The Khaibit can see into the Ka and Khat and is a kind of shape-shifting artist, creating mythic and dream reality from the shadows it receives from the spiritual bodies. It does not behold the reality of the spiritual world, but attempts to put together a story and vision based on the shadows it receives. Discovering one's mythic reality and its guiding archetype is but one step in an unfolding revelation of who one is.

The guiding archetype one's Khaibit holds must be confronted if the myth is to be altered to reach the level of the reality of the spiritual bodies (Sahu and Khu). The personal myth's symbolic form must be destroyed to transcend the unreality of impermanence. If the Khaibit attempts this confrontation and battle without access to the powers of the Sahu, the person may experience severe harm. It will feel as if one is under attack, for it one identifies with the Khaibit and lower bodies (Ka, Khat) there is no doubt that the world views (mythic reality) and self image they hold will be destroyed in the process. Sometimes even the physical body is destroyed if the identification with a limited mythic reality is strong enough. The subconscious and unconscious positive and negative powers will battle until more constant contact is made with the soul and spiritual bodies.

The KHAIBIT is the unconscious "shadows"

One of the keys to the process of contact of the lower bodies to the spiritual bodies is through another psycho mental body that does not hold the shadowy unconscious role—the Ab. The Ab is the conscience as mediator and must be made clear to reflect the truth of the Ba (soul). The Ab is more like a mirror than a shadow (like the Khaibit), but it is not the truth of reality of the spiritual bodies. The Ab, as conscience, is our perception of reality influenced by wisdom, experience and subconscious understanding. We make judgements depending on our conscience. The wisdom and understanding of the spiritual bodies must be the source of perception and discernment of the Ab to see clearly through illusions, projections, and confusion. If the Ab is not clear, it cannot reflect the light of the spiritual bodies lucidly. It will make judgements based on the influences of the Khaibit and Ka who may have their deep unconscious and subconscious agendas (desires and fears).

The conscience has the possibility of complete peace and equanimity amidst the ups and downs of life. Without learning equanimity and peace, there is reaction, agitation, and rebirth. The Ab dispenses justice to itself. If it is clouded with reaction (fear, hatred, resentment, jealousy) it pronounces judgements on others wherein it must reexperience the same lessons. As the Seat of the Soul in the heart, the Ba decides what we have to reexperience (fate, rebirth) or whether we have more freedom of choice.

Let us look at the diverse influences from other bodies reflected by the Ab. Receptive to the Sahu (spiritual body yet to be discussed) the Ab receives wisdom and understanding of limits.

Reflective of the Life Force (Sekhem) the Ab regulates our strength, resilience, and power.

Reflective of the soul (Ba), the Ab models its conscience on soul purpose. This is direct inspiration, the inner voice of the soul. Transmitting and reflective to the Khaibit, the Ab can discipline the aberrant psycho mental mythic reality according to its conscience.

The Khaibit is the rectifier of emotions, but the Ab rectifies the Khaibit if the unconscious is open to becoming conscious. It will not be open if it is defending something in the unseen shadows of its archetype, that is, if it is in denial.

The AB is the conscience, which reflects other subtle bodies

Transmitting and reflective of the Ka, the Ab can alter the subconscious self-image and body-image by reflecting back any illusions, which simultaneously reflects the true immortal nature of the soul (Ba).

The Ba is the soul, which knows its purpose, but the rest of our being may not be in alignment with it. Each soul evolves in its power and archetypal reality or purpose, but it has an immortal essence, and may express itself in innumerable lives—past, future or parallel.

The Ba, along with the Khaibit and Ab, is a psycho mental vehicle, but it strongly resonates to and is supported by the spiritual bodies. In fact the Ba resides in the Sahu, the most creative of the spiritual bodies.

The Ba is the soul, which knows its purpose

The Sekhem is life force that runs through all subtle channels and all bodies. The resonance of the inner life with the cosmos enables oneness of the heart-mind (soul) with the Ba of the cosmos. Through deep rhythmic breath, the Sekhem is harmonized and increased. Known as kundalini, the Sekhem is an awakening power that can activate all bodies. When the Sekhem activates the Ba and is inspired by the spiritual bodies, one's unique soul can come into alignment with the universal Ba (the soul of God).

The Sekhem is the vital energy of the kundalini

The Ba breaking through the unconscious shadows of the Khaibit

It is in the spiritual body of the Sahu that white magic occurs—for with the Sahu's activation we become conscious of our own "Neter" (god-goddess), our teacher/mentor from the invisible planes. Participation in the realities created by our guide-teacher is a privilege open to those with conscious spiritual aspirations. To activate the Sahu, we use words of power, mudras, sacred dance, healing, methods of using subtle energy, shape-shifting, metamorphosis, alchemy and all ways of accessing gods and goddesses (archetypal intelligences and energies). Through the mystical experience of the Ba, the Ba is dissolved into the essence of the Sahu's world.

High spiritual work involves working with the Sahu world and Sahu body. Then all the lower bodies are involved in sacred movement, in art and the art of life, for the Sahu dreams the essence of the myth that is our soul purpose. We must work in a deep inner way to access this dream; otherwise we are cut off from our real soul purpose that gives life meaning. The most important work in interaction with the Neters (archetypes: gods and goddesses) is being present with the cosmic drama while not being attached.

The Sahu involves all the lower bodies in sacred art

The true Christ-like (Osiris-like) spiritual body is the Khu, which lives in close proximity to the Neters, the representatives of God in the celestial realms.

The Ba resides within the Sahu and yet reflects the Khaibit

Paranormal phenomena of questioning the consensus reality of any given culture brings one into a higher cognition and alignment with the Sahu. The spiritual bodies connect to the awesome numinous realm and open us to an intensity and range of feelings and energies that are both beautiful and horrific. To align with the Sahu we must be free of all limited status quo "normal" identifications.

The Khu continues the work of the Sahu and becomes an adept along the continuum of consciousness, becoming able to experience states otherwise given only by the grace of God or his/her celestial representatives. When the Khu receives the Sekhem power, the kundalini rises into the head and beyond, altering the brain and increasing one's illumination and self-realization.

The Khu is the most subtle of all the nine bodies. It is the subtlety of the light of nothingness. The ground of being is, for the Khu, in the Void, the Source of all. Through dissolution in the mystical experience the lower bodies may reorganize in an alchemical transformation. This is destroying the personal myth and coming into the cosmic myth.

Mystical Experiences: The Dark Night of the Soul

Mystical experiences exist in oriental traditions known as Satori, Nirvana, and Samadhi. These experiences are more revelations than experiences. They expose the whole person (except the Ba, the soul, and the spiritual bodies) to dangers of dread, despair, confusion, the powers of self-will and chaos. The Dark Night of the Soul is not a dark night for the soul (or spiritual bodies) but a fear in the lower bodies losing their power and mythic reality.

The real resolution to this fear is to vow to activate and stand in all nine bodies. Subsequent to integration and wholeness, the Khu's awareness of the nonhuman realms is terrifying to the physical and psycho mental bodies (except for those with a clear conscience and aligned soul). For the Khu can "see" the divine and demonic beings. If the other bodies are not integrated, they become terrified, suicidal, confused, and flung into despair, or agony.

Integration

When all nine bodies are differentiated (activated) and integrated, we begin to master ourselves and contribute to the evolutionary scheme by teaching, inner work, healing or other initiatory functions in communications, government, agriculture or other professions. Such a being will be recognized by his/her presence or power, the conscious awareness of his/her destiny or "myth," his/her method of speaking to the Khaibit (deep unconscious, shadow) and physical body more than one's conscious self-image. Such people will have a clear dedication to bringing order out of chaos, exhibit humility in regard to the world and have an inspired link with the celestial world. They can be recognized by their stability of devotion to God and the unceasing unfoldment and manifestation of order out of chaos in their lives.

Egyptian tantra is a practice aimed at the reunion of a person with absolute reality through the realization that duality comes from Unity and must return to it. By integrating the male and female qualities in our lower bodies, we reach the state of the One. Neters (archetypal gods and goddesses) emanate from the One. And Neters have a male and female principle within them. It is the archetypal masculine and feminine that are to be reunited within us so that we can unite with the One. Therefore tantra (uniting male and female principles) is an inherent part of the Egyptian sacred understanding.

The Khu resides with Prime Source in the Eternal Light

Notes on Cultural Perspectives of Light Bodies

What many sacred texts have in common is a trinity of positive, negative, and neutral and diverse levels of consciousness that are an inherent part of the light bodies. The Egyptian Nine Bodies has a trinity on the physical, psycho-mental and spiritual levels. The Samkhya and Yoga teachings have the three qualities of *tamas, sattva* and *rajas*, as part of *Prakriti*, the changing, creative world, which then manifests as the three categories of elements, connotative and cognitive senses.

In the Chinese philosophy of the *Secret of the Golden Flower*, the division of the Tao into *yin* and *yang*, and *ming* and *hsing*, descending into *po* and *hun* are the polarities, like tamas and rajas of the Yoga schools. The way of returning to the One, or the Golden Flower, or, in the Yoga schools of *Purusha* (pure absolute spirit) is always through the central or mediating place, corresponding with the *sattva* guna.

In *Kabbalah*, the three pillars are similar polarities with the sephiroth of Kether, Tiphereth, and Yesod, residing in the central pillar.

The kundalini energy of Yoga, being the *Sekhem* of the Egyptian texts, and the *Speirema* of John's *Apocalypse*, is the life-force, the awakener, often identified as a serpent. The shadow, the subconscious and unconscious are to be subsumed, cleared, and purified, so that all the light bodies are aligned, and resonating in harmony.

In Yoga the three main canals (*nadis*) are the *ida* to the left, the *pingala* to the right, and the *sushumna* in the center. When practising Yoga, *prana* (identified with breath) or vital energy runs through the *ida* and *pingala*. *Prana* is the vehicle on which is carried *citta*, the psyche's willful, emotional, and mental activity. *Citta*, activated through the two canals by *prana*, puts us in interaction with the outer world, moving in thousands of different ways.

Yoga brings the *citta* to flow back through the two canals to meet at the perineum into the central canal and up to the *brahmarandhra* at the sagittal suture of the head. It is in the central channel at the *brahmarandhra* that cosmic consciousness is reflected, wherein the essential *bodhi* (illumination) is born. The first principle is then lived, bringing about a cessation of *citta's* movements whereupon illumination flares up. This reintegration with the first principle takes place in three phases, localized in three chakras and assimilated into the three bodies of the Buddha (the Nirmanakaya, the Sambogakaya, and the the Dharmakaya). The *citta* becomes purified until it vanishes in a supreme beatitude of *sahaja*, the Absolute in all of us. The Primordial Man-Woman is eternally present, but is now revealed.

The Egyptian vantage of nine light bodies is only one among several from diverse sacred world traditions. What I wish to emphasize here is that the light bodies and auras relate to states of consciousness and modes of life. What we think, how we feel, what we say and do are directly related to our chakras and light bodies and our state of being on all levels. This book is designed to assist the reader-participant with being more aware of the colors, patterns, symbols, and qualities of life in action that are resonant with them to the greater purpose of being one with the One.

Chapter Two:
OVERVIEW OF LIGHT BODIES

There are anywhere from five (Tibetan Buddhist) to nine (Egyptian) chakras or light bodies in various cultures. Chakras are the vortices or spinning wheels that transmit the codes of light out into the world, and that receive cosmic energy and light into the body. Chakras are the mediators between the eternal light codes and energy flow in various subtle levels in human bodies.

Isaac Newton, in 1729, first described the chakra energies or the auric field, for the modern world. His awareness did not come from ancient wisdom, but from an electromagnetic light that is subtle, vibrating, and elastic. The electromagnetic nature of the human body is now under greater research, but there is no doubt that it exists. In the 1930s, Dr. Harold Saxton Burr researched what he called "L-fields." These fields, measurable by science, are the energy counterpart of what I am calling light codes. Energy is the mover and means for light codes to become manifest.

In H.R. Nagendra's model of the *Unified Subtle Energy in Human Systems*,[1] energy is stored at the base chakra and flows upward, and is used by basic autonomic activities around the heart chakra. This subtle energy is usually used up in sense pleasures, emotional reactions, and thinking actions in the head. All spiritual practices can reverse this loss of energy in a body system, and bring about illumination and regeneration.

How Chakras Work

The electromagnetic field of the body comes about through the spinning of our chakras. And what signals them to spin, how fast and in what way? Light codes. Light codes are the numeric indexes of color, sound, and vibration. Color and harmonics are, therefore, key to our light bodies. Magnetism is the director of electrical energy and therefore closer to the light codes than energy is. It is my intuition that magnetism is intermediary between electrical energy and light codes and transmits symbols as information. Magnetism is a polarity-based phenomenon, but one that is complete in itself, for there are both positive and negative poles in magnetism; whereas electricity uses one or the other.

In brief, codes are received from above and below the human body and they step down or modify to resonate with the light codes within the human body. The earth's codes and energy comes up through the feet into the base or root chakra. Cosmic light codes are received by the upper chakras from stars and subtle grids of three dimensions as well as higher dimensions.

CHAKRAS

The chakras are vortices through which light codes are distributed by means of energy. The chakras make the aura appear brighter, grayer, darker or with interference, depending on how clearly the codes are being received and transmitted. A pale, but clear color indicates a clear chakra.

The light-codes entering the crown chakra are sometimes called rays. The crown chakra, associated with the pineal, takes in light codes from the cosmos. The brow chakra, associated with the pituitary gland, functions like a prism, refracting the light codes and sending them into various chakras below. The pituitary is the master gland because it regulates the hormonal secretions of all the ductless glands, which are directly influenced by the light codes through the chakras.

Moving down into the throat chakra, associated with the thyroid gland, the light codes lower their frequency so that the codes from the cosmos can interact more easily with the various bodies. The pineal and the crown chakra resonate to the Sahu body; whereas the chakras above the head, resonate with the Khu body. At the throat, the Sekhem resonates and at the heart resides the Ba or soul.

At the throat the light codes are divided into three: the *rajas*, male, active side on the right; the *tamas*, female, passive side on the left and the *sattva*, neutral, harmonizing in the center. The three are resonant with the Yogic *ida, pingala* and *sushumna* canals. The Caduceus symbol is appropriate for these three channels: the double serpents, being the *ida* and *pingala* on each side and the central rod being the *sushumna* canal. The pine cone which sits atop the central canal in the Caduceus symbol resonates with the pineal and crown chakra, the vortex which receives the light-codes.

The heart chakra, associated with the thymus gland, is the crucible of transmutation. The heart chakra transmutes the codes coming up from the earth, through the feet and base chakra, and transmits the light codes coming down from the upper chakras. The thymus regulates the immune system. The heart chakra is the "seal of the soul." And the soul resides in the Sahu, which resonates with the light codes in the pineal gland, before being separated.

Coming down, the energy resonance becomes denser. The adrenal glands are activated at the solar plexus. The spleen, pancreas and liver—filtering glands and organs—are integral parts of the solar plexus chakra, resonant with the Ab body. At the second chakra, resonant with the gonads, the energy activates the sexual energies, which nourishes the whole body. The root chakra at the perineum is open to the codes from the earth through the feet.

The reverse process, coming from below upwards, the energy becomes more and more refined as it moves up the chakras: Substance, connections, and energy all activate light codes. When light codes are all activated from all chakras and centers, the aura is very brilliant and one is resonant with the One.

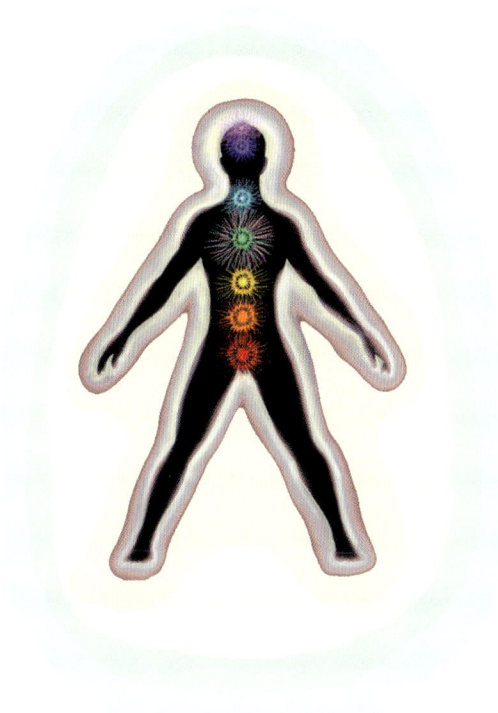

Chakras and Auric Field

The chakras are shown here as variously colored "lights" or vortices running vertically up the body; whereas the auric field, which radiates these same subtle energies, surrounds the physical body in various circumferential egg-like rings. Clarivoyants see various shapes, symbols, colors, and forms within the aura, which helps them read the aura. The depiction here is without symbols (light codes) as well as interference (blocks, wounds traumas etc.)

(right)

The Relation of a Chakra System to the Nine Egyptian Light Bodies

also giving keynotes to be discussed later

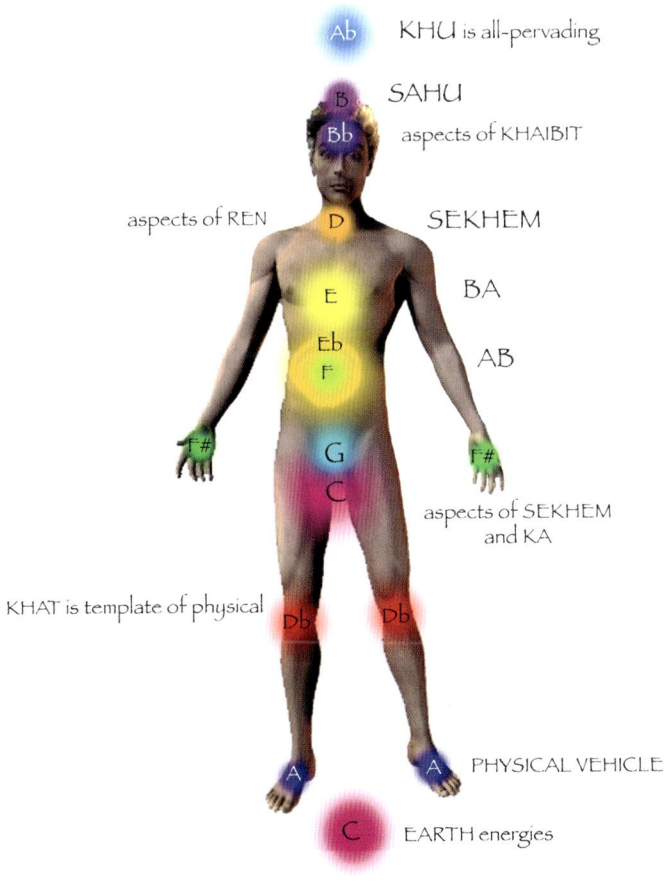

KHU is all-pervading

SAHU

aspects of KHAIBIT

aspects of REN

SEKHEM

BA

AB

aspects of SEKHEM and KA

KHAT is template of physical

PHYSICAL VEHICLE

EARTH energies

The Relationship of the Chakras to the Endocrine System

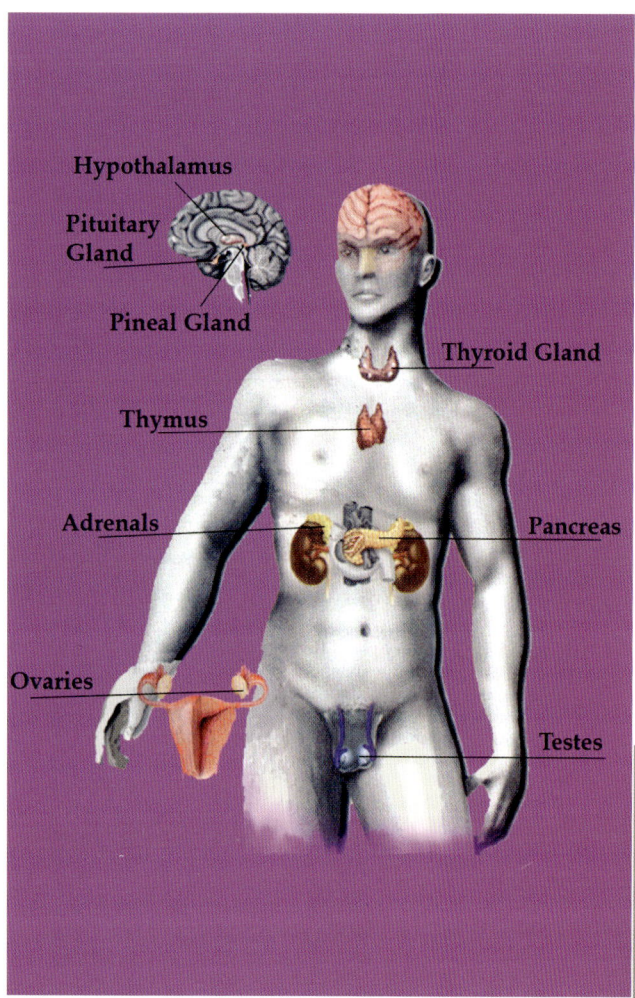

The chakras relate to the endocrine system of the physical body. The endocrine is influenced by the chakras, more than the other way around. The chakras are dynamic generators of energy flow, which are both receptive and transmissive. The chakras radiate colors and (to most people) inaudible "sounds" which make up the auric field of a person. In this book, the auric field is symbolized by *Robes of Light.*

Specific archetypes are transmitted through symbols within the auric field. Archetypes are primary patterns that are intermediary between the pure light codes and the energy and physical bodies. I am not so much talking only about psychological archetypes as Carl Jung does, but rather patterns that receive light codes and that direct the energy flow of physical phenomenon.

The endocrine system of the body is the chemical transducer of the subtle energies and light codes. Hormones are chemical messengers in the bloodstream affecting the metabolism of target cells, often located in another ogan. The endocrine glands secrete hormones directly into surrounding tissue fluids.

The nervous system and endocrine systems use complementary methods of communication, but both systems communicate through chemistry. Some chemicals work both as neurotransmitters and as hormones.

The endocrine system is a communication system between the chakras, which are vortices of energy, receptive to light codes, and the physical body.

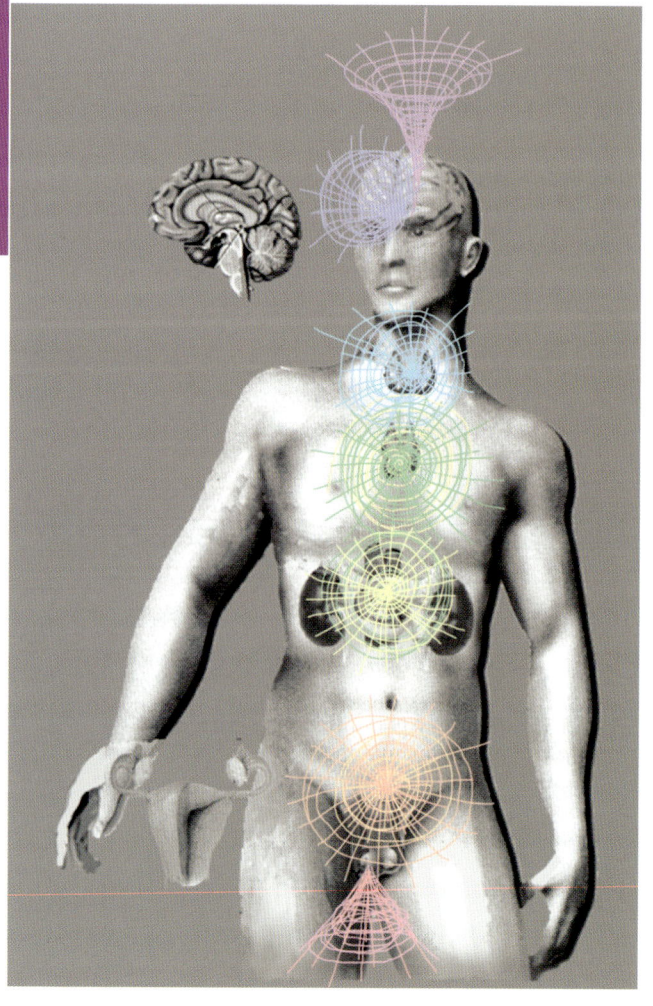

In general, we can say, based on ancient wisdom, that the human is a microcosm and that consciousness is a key of the transmission of light codes into energy flow, creating and maintaining the energy bodies. The macrocosm is not only the physical, scientifically measurable universe, but the higher consciousness universe, all the way to the stillpoint of Prime Source, from which all light codes (the programs for creation) issue. The macrocosm has chakras, or energy vortices also, but that is another subject.

Another generalization, based on the ancient sacred texts, is that enlightenment or a return to the One, is the complement of creation and evolution in its direction of energy flow. The spiritual practitioner has become manifest (through creation and evolution) and enlightenment (ascension, and regeneration) seeks to release separation, cease the outward flowing motion, cease dissipation and come to the stillpoint, one with the One. Sexual energy, becoming *kundalini* (*Speirema* of Greek, and *Paraclete* of Christian texts), instead of being released outwardly, is sent into a central subtle energy channel, where it rises into the highest chakras. It is by ceasing consciousness of all duality that this supreme awareness occurs.

The flow of light codes and energy through the chakras is key to health and well-being. Fears and anxieties as well as repression of sexual energy impede the flow of this subtle energy. This does not mean that sexual abandon leads to enlightenment, but rather that, as we learn to regulate our subtle energy, we learn to use cosmic and earth energies descending and ascending through the vortices of our chakras, to nurture ourselves and all of life. Enlightenment is also a transmutation of sexual energy. Creativity is a key process that enables the free-flow of subtle energy throughout our bodies and in interaction with other people and our environment.

The magnetic field of the energy body is a force field of resonances which likely communicates the information of light codes into energy flow through symbols.

Symbols are consciousness-patterns as a language, intermediary between the higher dimensional worlds, the psycho-mental and physical realms.

below:
CROP CIRCLE, Avebury Trusloe, near Avebury, Wiltshite, reported July 22, 2000, showing a form of a magnetic field.

Bibliography

Baba, Bangali, *The Yogasutra of Patanjali*, Motilal Banarsidass, Delhi, Varanasi, Patna, 1976

Bailey, Alice, *The Rays and the Initiations*, New York: Lucis Publishing Company, 1972

Becker, Robert O. and Gary Selden, *The Body Electric: Electromagnetism and the Foundation of Life*, New York, William Morrow, 1985

Blavatsky, H.P. *The Secret Doctrine*, Pasadena, CA: Theosophical University Press, 1974

Burr, Harold Saxton, *The Fields of Life: Our Links with the Universe*, New York: Ballatine, 1972

Clark, R.T. Rundle, *Myth and symbol in Ancient Egypt*, Tames and Hudson, London, 1959

Eliade, Mircea, *Patanjali and Yoga*, tr. by Markmann, Funk & Wagnalls, New York, 1969

Faulkner, Raymond, tr. *The Egyptian Book of the Dead/ The Book of Going Forth by Day*, Chronicle Books, San Francisco, 1994

Freke, Timothy and Gandy, Peter, The Hermetica, Jeremy P. Tarcher/Putnma, New York, 1999

Gray, William G. *Concepts of Qabalah*, Sangreal Sodality Series, volume 3, Samuel Weiser, Inc, 1984

Kilmer, Walter J, *The Human Aura,* New York: Citadel Press, 1965

Krippner, Stanley and Rubin, Daniel, editors, *Energies of Consciousness,* New York: Gordon and Breach Science Publishers, 1975

Masters, Robert, *The Goddess Sekhmet*, Amity House, Amity, N.Y. 1988

Motoyama with Rande Brown, *Science and the Evolution of Consciousness*: Chakras, Ki, and Psi

Nartoomid, Maia Christine, *The Sanctuary of Kheper-Ra and the Golden Winged Scarab*, p. 61-72 *Temple Doors, Doctrine of Sacred Inner Mysteries*, Issue 4-97

Reich, Wilhelm, *The Discovery of the Orgone*, New York: Orgone Institute Press, 1948

Robinet, Isabelle, *Taoist Meditation*, State University of New York Press, New York, 1993

Schwaller de Lubicz, R.A., *Sacred Science: The King of Pharaonic Theocacy*, Inner Tradtions International, Rochester, VT. 1982

[1]Srinivasan, T.M., ed. *Energy Medicine Around the World*, p. 71-81, Phoenix, AZ, Gabriel Press, 1988

Schwarz, Jack, *Human Energy Systems*, New York, E. P. Dutton, 1980

Tansley, Davide, *The Raiment of Light: A Study of the Human Aura*, New York: Methuen, Arcana Division, 1987

Wilhelm, Richard, *The Secret of the Golden Flower*, tr. Wilhelm Baynes, Harcourt, Brace & World, Inc, New York, 1962

In the next parts of this book, we will explore a sixfold and then a twelvefold model of cosmos and human energy body through twenty-four fictional human characters, representing archetypes.

Chapter Three:
CREATIVITY, CYCLES, AND PSYCHIC ATTRACTORS
Creativity

Light bodies are kept pure and flowing through creativity. Everyone has creative capacity. You can discover where in the creativity cycle you may be flowing or stuck, strong or weak and thus make corrections in your life. Your light bodies will become more purified as you work creatively on all levels.

In creativity we begin with *receptivity* and openness to spirit—a state of pure being. Being receptive, we receive *inspiration* which might also be called intuition. When the spirit comes in we activate our *imagination*, In order to discover how the *inspiration* might be applied to life. When we have imagined it from many angles, more and more spiritual energy enters all our subtle bodies until we are impelled to take *action*. *Action* begins the yang, centrifugal light half of the cycle. What was interior becomes exterior. And *action manifests*—whether it be a business, a garden or a tool, the manifest phase is most externalized. After manifestation there is *release*—giving away or using what we have manifested. Release is the last phase of the light half of the cycle. From complete release, *receptivity* is possible again.

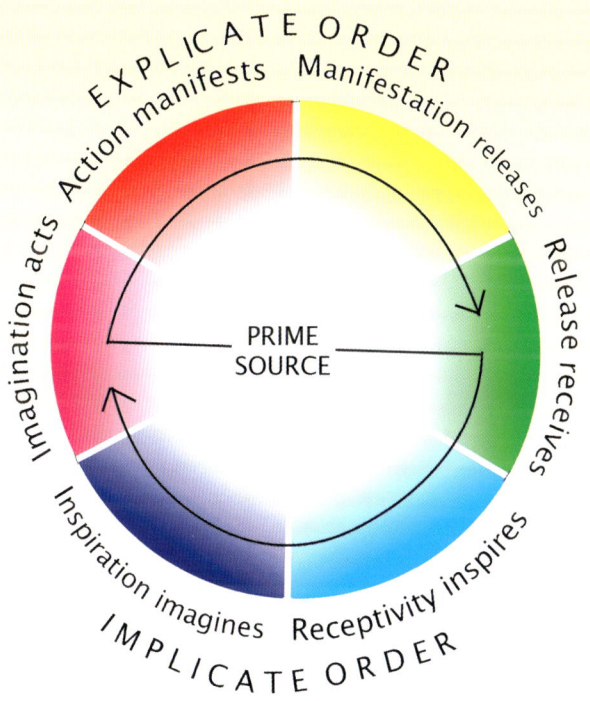

Creativity Cycle

The creativity cycle helps define how the subjective and objective worlds are also part of a cycle. The outer world, beginning with *imagination acts* and moving to *action manifests* and *manifestation releases*, reveals the explicate or objective. The inner world, beginning with *release receives* and moving to *receptivity inspires*, and *inspiration imagines* reveals how the subjective is as much a part of reality as the objective. Prime Source is the invisible source within both the inner and outer realms.

Some intuitive people are stronger on the inner, yin half and have trouble taking their inner life into action and manifestation. Other, more yang types of people, take action often without deeply finding inspiration and imagination. They need receptivity and opening to the inner life.

Scientists measure only the objective half, with the exception of some phenomenological studies of reports from people in deep inner states.

Creativity is a communion through the heart where all memories are revealed in the fires of loving imagination.

Creativity is finding symbols from the deep mysteries to reveal meaning amidst a world of shifting forms.

Creative Vision is an internal sacrament in communion with Prime Source and a rising into action in the world.

Creativity brings us to see the correspondence of things and find meaning and wholeness amidst sentient fragments.

Creativity is the essential nature of the Divine Human—the potential within us all.

Creating is as natural as flowing water. The macrocosm flows in the microcosm like flax through a sieve. Stretching our capacity on physical, emotional and mental levels allows more of reality to flow through.

The creativity cycle is a sixfold cycle consisting of a yin and yang, dark and light polarity. The yang, light (magenta, red, yellow) side is more outward and the yin, dark (green turquoise, blue) side is more inward. This is not a value judgement, but an understanding of how polarity creates a cycle.

I work with an expanded sixfold cycle that enables you to understand a given archetypal phase within a greater cycle. Each of the six phases breaks into two and a twelvefold pattern results. The keynotes given are those that correspond to the keynotes of the chakras given on page 16.

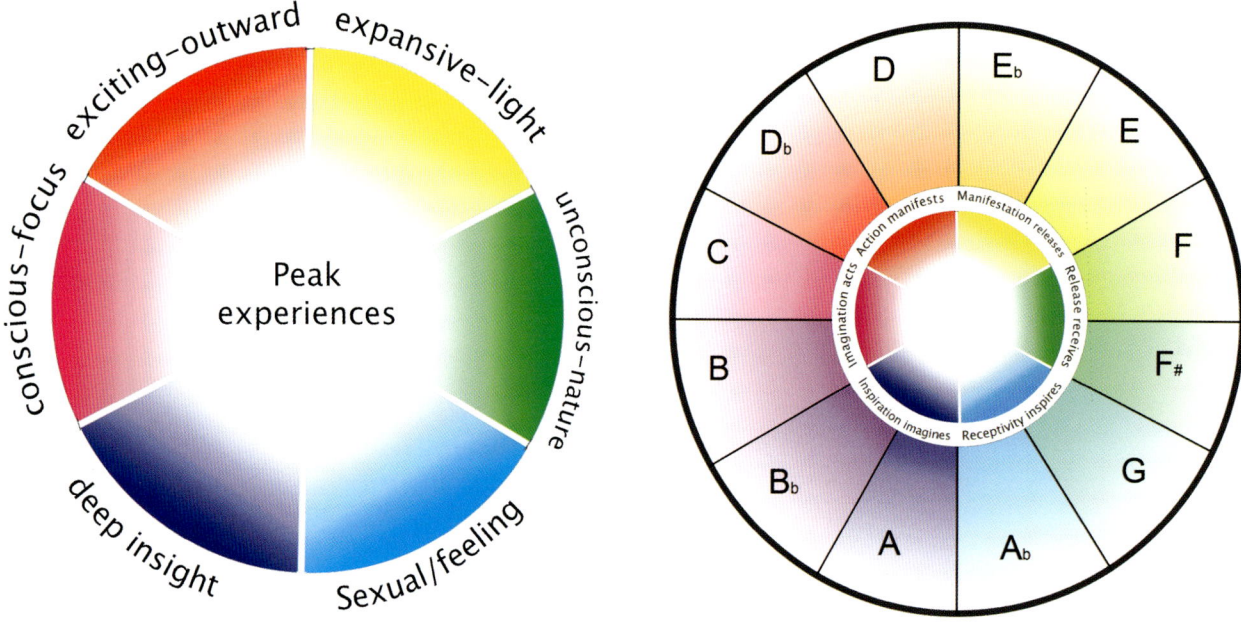

In the creativity cycle, *release receives* introduces the yin, feminine, more receptive side as the Implicate Order, and *imagination acts* introduces the yang, masculine, active side as the Explicate Order. (See diagram on previous page).

Within a twelvefold cycle there are two qualities in each of the sixfold phases. Look at the image on the next page and see the patterns of correspondence. The Psychic Attractors (forms) are called morphotypes in my book, Sophia's Body

In general, the twelvefold cycle has the following qualities:

Imagination Acts: B and C (Pisces and Aries)
The action of codes or seeds in fertile ground
B: Manure or soil, decay, fertile ground, symbolized by the unpredictable forms
C: Seed, code, light of consciousness, symbolized by the point

Action Manifests: Db and D (Taurus and Gemini)
Accumulation of matter that branches out
Db: Step by step progress, new ideas and steady devotion to them, symbolized by the step
D: Respiration, transformation, exploration, multiple views, symbolized by the branch

Manifestation Releases: Eb and E (Cancer and Leo)
Vortices that radiate out in explosive release
Eb: Generation, energy flow, creation, juicing up ideas, symbolized by the spiral
E: Explosive release in radiation, symbolized by the radial

Release Receives: F and F# (Virgo and Libra)
Feedback in balance and alignment
F: Discernment and feedback from within and from others, symbolized by the torus or loop
F#: Balancing the inner and outer, moving into action, symbolized by the column

Receptivity Inspires: G and Ab (Scorpio and Saggitarrius)
Inner movement and transformation
G: Movement from outside moving inward, symbolized by the wave
Ab: Return of codes to source, symbolized by the diamond

Inspiration Imagines: A and Bb (Capricorn and Aquarius)
Substance interconnected by consciousness field
A: Creation of matter, and protective membrane, symbolized by the sphere or circle
Bb: Grid lines of consciousness interconnecting throughout space, symbolized by the grid

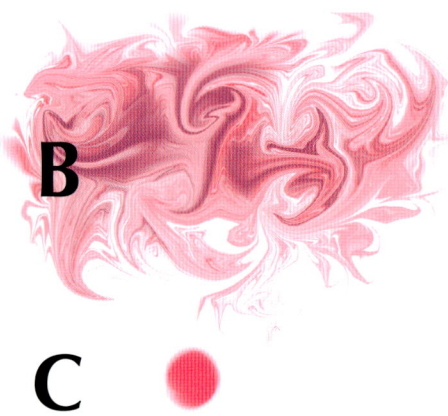

B

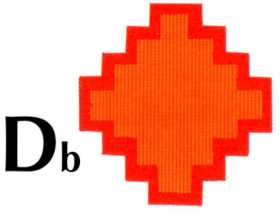

C

Correlations of the Twelvefold Cycle

tone	color	form	sign
B	lavender	unpredictable	Pisces
C	magenta	point	Aries

Imagination acts in the creativity cycle. The dissolution resulting from the break down of all pattern in the unpredictable form implies a transition from the inner world to the outer world. It involves moving through chaos to a new light, a seed-idea. I use the tone of C for the initiating function of the seed idea or code because C as 256 cycles per second reduces to number 1. Symbolized by the Divine Eye, this function is centered in Eternal Light and the eye that sees inner light.

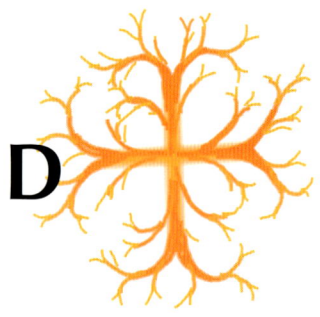

Db

D

tone	color	form	sign
Db	red	step	Taurus
D	orange	branch	Gemini

Action manifests in the creativity cycle. The step represents a slow, constant, perservering process. It is an accumulation of mass, of matter and correlates with Taurus, an earth sign. The function of the branch is distribution through transforming connections. You might visualize it as the media, communication and transport systems. The branch correlates with Gemini and the tone of D. The overall symbol is the lotus as a fulfillment in manifestation.

Eb

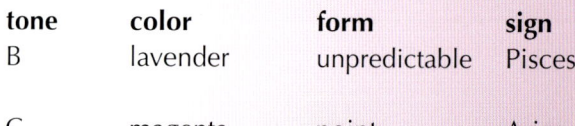

E

tone	color	form	sign
Eb	gold	spiral	Cancer
E	yellow	radial	Leo

Continuing the active, yang side of the cycle, we have two psychic attractors of the spiral/vortex and the radial. The spiral, correlating with Eb and the zodiacal sign of Cancer, generates energy, and the radial, correlating with E and Leo, radiates it out in explosive release. *Manifestation releases* is as essential as *inspiration imagines* on the opposite side of the cycle. Giving with trust is a key attitude. The overall symbol is the Caduceus. We need here to be active, but then to let go and let God.

Correlations of the Twelvefold Cycle

tone	color	form	sign
F	lime green	torus/loop	Virgo
F#	green	column	Libra

F

Release receives in the creativity cycle. The tone-forms of F and F# are like a magnetic field that continuously turns inside out through an axis. Symbolized often as tree, spear, egg (torus) in various myths *release receives* is a time when we must surrender and yet be centered. Maintaining meditation or a means of balance is essential, for during this time we are being cleared of unconscious shadows. Dumbfounded by life-changing events, we open up to possibilities out of the unconscious, and drink of the elixir of immortality from the divine receptacle of the grail cup.

F#

tone	color	form	sign
G	cyan blue	wave	Scorpio
Ab	blue	diamond	Sagittarius

G

Receptivity inspires in the creativity cycle. The wave carries the codes and maintains energy flow as a transmitter of inspiration. The diamond is a receptacle that mirrors and receives codes as a way of transforming them into higher and higher dimensions. In this phase we need to be open, receptive and yet awake and aware. Meditation more than sleep is the answer here. The overall symbol is the wings of Isis or Ra, the wings of inspiration, the flight of the inner light.

Ab

tone	color	form	sign
A	blue-violet	sphere	Capricorn
Bb	purple	grid	Aquarius

Inspiration imagines in the creativity cycle. The sphere represents a boundary, a membrane that, at once, protects and creates substance from within.

The grid is just the opposite: for it interconnects in a globally expansive way and has no boundaries. The imagination has no boundaries through the grid and yet inspiration may be creative and specific. The overall symbol is the thunderbolt signifying inner awakening that rebounds throughout space.

A

Bb

Chapter Four:
SOUL PATTERNS AND ARCHETYPES

Getting acquainted with the psychic attractors of the twelvefold cycle is helpful to understanding the unfoldment of inner and outer events in your life. We have just laid the foundation for qualities that I am calling archetypes in this book. Archetypes are primary patterns that run through various dimensions. That means this twelvefold cycle, (corresponding with colors, keynotes, creativity functions, and psychic attractors), is an archetypal pattern that runs through all nine Egyptian light bodies. Each archetype is a different, unique way to move through the initiations we will explore in this book.

One way to experience the archetypes is to learn the qualities of the zodiacal signs, which may or may not be familiar to you. The twlevetone scale in music may be familiar to you instead. Most everyone, except the blind and color blind, know the colors. The forms (that I call psychic attractors), are familiar all through Nature.

Consider that you find the point in seeds and in the pupil of your eye. You find the step in any kind of gradation. The branch is not only in trees, but in lungs and blood vessels. Look for the spiral in galaxies, water vortices and generators. The radial is clearly in the sun and also flowers. Find the torus or loop in any kind of feedback system. The column is in the trunks of trees and in your legs. Find the wave, not only in the ocean, but in the whole electromagnetic spectrum. The diamond combines triangles, which you can find in gems and grids. The sphere is any enclosure that protects, and the grid itself is not only in bee hives, but in matrices, around planets, and in your mind.

This simple universal language is not difficult, but may be unfamiliar to many adults. This universal language is truly universal, not by custom or familiarity, but because it is everywhere available for those with minds and senses. Color, sound, movement, form, and number are the universal languages that children know as soon as they move, open their eyes and ears and begin to count.

If you learn this simple language you will be much freer of cultural conventions (which are interesting, but changeable) and rest your value system and world view on a substantial ground of Nature's laws in interaction with human perception. In this chapter I will introduce the concept of a psychic attractor, relating the twelve archetypes to psychological types.

An attractor in Chaos Theory is a region of phase space that attracts a system to it. Phase space has many variables that help describe a system's movement. Two cycles interacting can produce a torus, like electric and magnetic currents, 180° to each other. A torus is a two cycle attractor. The smaller cycle may be integral, in which case it returns in phase with its origin, or it may be fractional and continue to generate new cycles infinitely. Observe that the attractors have shapes. They are symbols in archetypal space as attractors are regions of phase space.

Analogously, I am introducing "psychic attractors," the equivalent of emotional-mental realms to the forms of Chaos Theory. Each of the "psychic attractors" is clustered around an archetype, which means "primary pattern." As archetypes, they may be identified with specific characteristics or qualities of people. In this chapter I am introducing you to twelve qualities through the dispositions, facial qualities as well as life-styles of different people. They also have different soul patterns, and as they move through the intiations, you will learn more about the psychic attractors as well as about the nine Egyptian light bodies. I have given them names to identify them, but they are typically demonstrating the twelve archetypes we are exploring in this book, as different archetypal "styles" of moving through the nine initiations.

Among our characters, there is a male and female version of each archetype and you may find yourself identifying with one or more characters, which may help you to know yourself.

THE POINT—tone of C, create codes

The **single-point attractor** is highly focussed and charged, creative and spiritual at once. Examples are in the DNA of the nucleus of cells, quasars in galaxies, and eternal light of stars. Why does a pendulum with resistance come to a center? Why are all the forces of a plant constellated in a single seed? Codes are sources as patterns of information.

The eternal light of stars, and creativity in cultures are examples of this psychic attractor. The species codes of plants and animals and Planck quanta on the subatomic level also demonstrate the single-point attractor.

This attractor manifests as codes, symbols or light. In humans, it is highly internal and of high vibrations. It exists in the matrix of everything that exists as a code or pattern of its potential. Sometimes it is called an *atoma*, or central seed-atom of a planet, sun, or even a stone.

Psychologically, people who have a dominance of the point attractor are highly intelligent, able to understand paradox, and can see into the higher potential of things, situations, or people. They can clarify an idea quickly and with great penetration and therefore make good leaders.

Symbol: The Divine Eye

Ariel

is intense, focussed and loves to initiate projects. She may have some difficulty in following through on things she initiates, but she holds the codes for high creativity. Others can be inspired purely by her presence. She brings inspiration down from the highest reaches of heaven, but may be impatient and even angry if her inspiration is not perceived.

Shawn

is intelligent and carries powerfully focussed energy. He can recognize common patterns in very diverse images instantly. Everything is in the NOW for Shawn, for essentially time does not exist in his consciousness. Yet he can bring ideas into action when necessary. He loves hiking in the mountains and is very good at designing and writing when inspired.

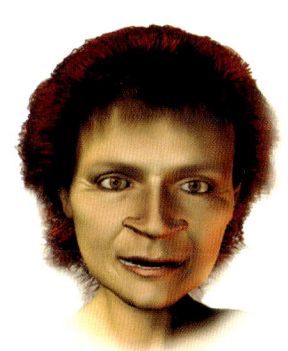

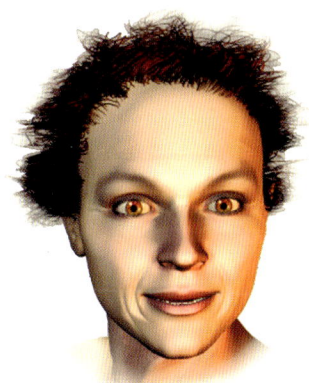

Use the single-point attractor when you need focus and also when praying or meditating. This attractor is most attuned to Source and Spirit. You do not need to understand so much as give wholehearted single-pointed focus to whatever you are pursuing.

THE STEP—tone of Db, maintain substance

The Step is the accumulative and incremental Step-down or Step-up attractor. The function of *maintaining substance* holds accretion, addition, mass and weight. Examples are the gravitational force of planets, the atomic weight of atomic elements, building in a culture and the physical body of a human. Other examples are the cell walls of plants, animal body types, and habitats of ecology. All of these have qualities of mass, accretion, slow change and physical structures. Qualities of this archetype are slowness, weightiness, and material.

Ratios of steps correspond to this psychic attractor. Use it to hold your ground, and to accumulate mass or money. Progress in a consistent direction is one of this psychic attractor's qualities.

Psychologically the step attractor relates to qualities of patience, perserverence, and ability to sustain a project to its completion. Not the most sensitive qualities, but people who are part of the Step "Tribe" can step-up or step-down any situation with grounded suggestions for manifestation.

Symbol: The Stepped Mountain.

Frank

is a rough and ready type of character who is very lovable and patient. He takes a step-by-step approach to anything he takes an interest in and always gets it done. He can maintain farms, households, autos, or other machinery. He is also very good at finances, and insurance of all kinds. He is reliable and steady, often engaging painstaking effort to accomplish anything he sets his mind to.

Elizabeth

is kind-hearted and loves the Earth. You will often find her in the garden, planting or caring for her vegetable garden. She is happy having a home to take care of and invites friends in occasionally to see her recent sculptures. She is very good with her hands, and is perservering in any project she begins, such as collages, or wood-carving. She cares about security and money, but only as a means to an end she values.

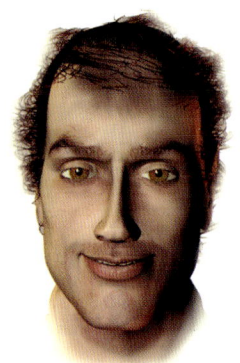  

Use the step psychic attractor when you need steady persistance and perserverence to accomplish or endure something. It helps to cure impatience or unreliability. Good for stability and maintaining resources for a certain goal.

THE BRANCH—tone of D, transform connection

The Branch is an attractor that reaches a critical point where connection is unstable and new connections are made. Two stable attractors split off from one. For example, bees split off from a hive to create a new hive. There is a critical point where the population becomes unstable and splits in two. In this way, populations go up and down. In psychology, it can be a splitting into multiple personalities if the core attractor of the soul is separated from. In physics, it is the splitting of matter and anti-matter. In plants this attractor is branching. In the lungs, it is respiration by use of branched bronchial tubes by the distribution of oxygen through two branching systems, lungs and vessels.

This attractor may also be seen in the distribution of goods. It can be an expression of the soul into complexity that is all connected to the monad or central soul. By transforming connection, one extends, communicates and distributes. In life expression, it is interest of many fields.

In a positive psychology it is multiple interests and abilities. The negative form is a splitting of soul and personality. The positive form is from an integration of personality to soul. Thus the soul has integral expression through the personality. The branch represents growth as well as division.

Symbols: Tree of Life, Caduceus

Karen

has many interests and pursues them at great length. Sometimes she may get over-extended in branching out in too many ways. She is effective as a secretary, inventory person, and in communications, and sometimes has been on TV and radio stations. Karen is quick-witted, agile and very swift to change. It is not that she is unreliable, but that she is highly transformative in diverse ways and it is hard to keep track of what she is doing.

Morgan

is inventive and was a child prodigy. He has made new vehicles and tried to fly when he was a child. He now owns a company that has share-holders in his inventions and after innumerable trials, he is now very successful in not only getting his inventions patented, but in making money. He is taking an interest in foreign trade and methods of selling his inventions abroad. His challenge is that his girl friends and yes, even wives, have a hard time relating to such a self-absorbed inventor.

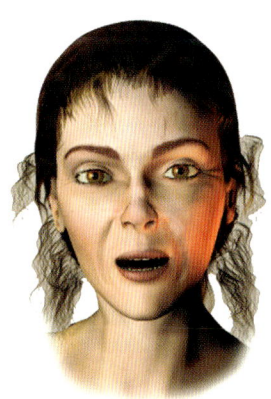
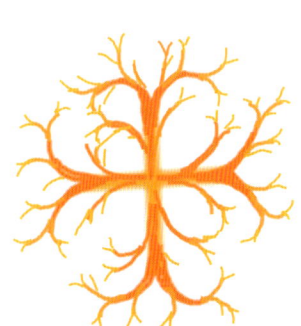
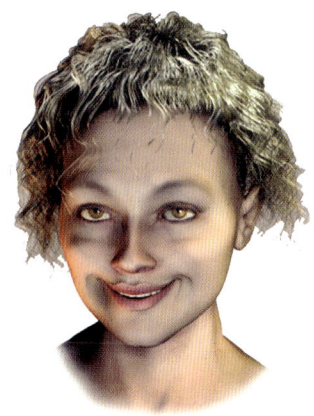

Use this psychic attractor for making significant choices and for effective communication. If there is a separation of some kind, look for a larger perspective on why a choice is being made—willingly or unwillingly. See how division sometimes helps with giving everyone space. Use this psychic attractor to find an effective distribution of goods or money.

THE SPIRAL—tone of Eb, create energy flow

This is the infinite vortex or spiral attractor. Spiralling motion creates a flow of current, of electricity, of water or any flowing substance. The overtone series in music is also an infinite vortex, for each octave returns to the same tone, but in a higher frequency.

In the spiral the point of origin has a clockwise or counterclockwise tendency, and each cycles from the same stillpoint where motion ceases. Examples are spinning up or down in leptons and also resonance at a distance in the subatomic realm.

The storage vortex has two stillpoints and the generating vortex has one, but the storage vortex always had a counter rotating twin. The generating vortex contains the counter rotating twins through the stillpoint.

The Hindu awareness of three types of energy flow is relevant: *rajas*, (active, fiery) *tamas* (slow, lethargic) and *sattva* (balanced, high spirited).

In consciousness, the *rajas* and *tamas* are polarities like the counter rotating spins—mediated by the *sattvic*, neutral stillpoint between them. Thus one may be overly active, driven outward by internal lack. Or one may be overly lethargic, sleepy, apathetic, driven inward into unconsciousness by confusion. Thus, creating flow is moving from within outward and from outward to within, in cycles. The stillpoint of neutrality of *sattva* is revealed in meditation as resonance with Prime Source.

Symbols: Tornado, Coils, Galaxy

Ricardo

loves to generate energy for groups, for he is passionate about initiating group projects that fulfill a community's needs. He is on many committees, but he mainly functions as a facilitator, for he sees many points of view and can synthesize them into a powerful direction for the benefit of all. He is sensitive to people's needs and yet takes care of his own.

His challenge is to not be overbearing in any way. He doesn't so much want to stand out, as to facilitate people being themselves. He also loves to swim and ride horses.

Jennifer

is extremely sensitive, and when she was younger, her sensitivity threw her into emotional turmoils. Now she has found that meditation has helped her equanimity amidst life's challenges, so she channels her pent-up energy into creative work. She dances and sings, and feels so dedicated to this expressive and harmonious work that she may be able to do it professionally.

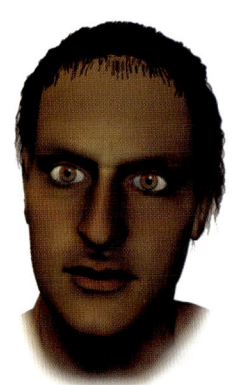  

The Vortex or Spiral psychic attractor can be used whenever you need to summon energy to fulfill a task you are devoted to. Always follow your joy when you visualize or summon this attractor, for it responds to feelings and heart-centeredness. You can use this psychic attractor by spinning, by drawing spirals, or by visualizing vortices in whatever part of you body needs energy.

THE RADIAL—tone of E, maintain codes

The radial is a point attractor moving in all directions. This implies it has an infinite source which links it to the point attractor of *create codes*. The maintenance part is the replication of the codes in radial lines from within outward.

Psychologically, it is unobstructed radiance. It is a vector, a ray, a linear probe. For codes to be maintained one needs exact replication like cell division. Cells express and maintain codes.

Why does light move in straight lines? Because the lines are already there! Space is a multi-dimensional invisible grid through which light travels from source—the point—of a star.

Psychologically, the radial is a broadcasting of soul. The shadow is nonexistent, the fixations are unscrewed and the expression is near absolute.

In the invisible world, the lines may go from outside in, but as maintenance, the lines are from inside outward. This implies a largely *rajas* or active, radiating nature. Many poets or musicians who express and then burn themselves out are of this nature.

Symbols: Sun, Flowers

Serafina

is a highly radiant being who, early in her years, had trouble understanding why so many people were attracted to her. Now she uses her presence to help people be more of themselves. She is so radiant that some people find her overbearing. Her spirit is high so that her main challenge is to enable her body, feelings and mind to elevate to where her spirit resides.

She has now become a painter, for in color she can broadcast her spiritual essence. Sometimes she paints abstracts, but they all stem from earlier paintings of brilliant flowers.

Francis

is a poet who also does carpentry to earn a living. Even his carpentry is poetry when he is given the chance to do cabinets, doors or objects that need refinement. His poetry is of the essence of life, for he sees the radiance of all living things. He uses exacting words to bring the essence of his subjects out in sounds as well as meaning.

He has done various spiritual practises, such as Kriya Yoga, Zen meditation, and Carmelite prayers, but he finds that traditions are too far removed from the spiritual essence of what he knows in his heart. Poetry speaks in divine sparks through words.

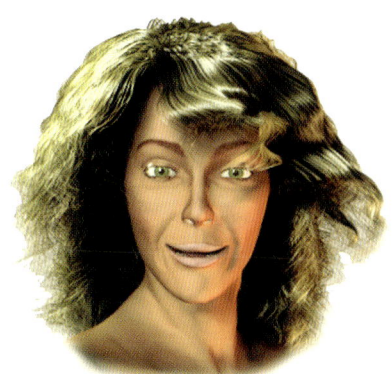

The Radial psychic attractor is best used to maintain spiritual dedication. Visualized in any part of the body, but most especially in the heart, it can access soul purpose and harmonize body and psyche more fully with spirit. Use this psychic attractor to broadcast your spiritual intent and to radiate to others the essence of your being.

THE LOOP OR TORUS—tone of F, transform substance

The Torus is a symbol of continuous inside-outing. Example are digestion and excretion through organic beings, and the feedback system of mother to child in embryogenesis. This psychic attractor is found in evacuation, excretion, and returning matter to the source of substance as the ground of being. There is a chemical transformation in digestion: acid breaks down into smaller components easier to assimilate. Multiplying a factor by itself produces feedback called iteration and nonlinearity. This attractor is also demonstrated in how the environment affects us and how we affect the environment in ecology. Find this psychic attractor in levels of nourishment: bacteria feed on our excretion and we feed on plants and animals. Manure for one may be nourishment to others.

The negative aspect of this attractor can be found in digestion illnesses: constipation, diarrhea or indigestion. All such diseases are related to substance not transformed or inability to take in and release. In anorexia, one is not hungry, as there is no interest in nourishment. On a psychological level anorexia relates to despair of being nourished, supported, and loved. Too fluid a cycle causes the inability to be receptive. There is no assimilation. Too fast a cycle doesn't transform substance. In health, this attractor helps with the ability of personality to transform and assimilate impressions and let useless ones go. Magnetism, which looks like a torus, is feedback from codes carried by electricity.

Symbols: Mobius, Torus

Franchesca

is very discriminative and sometimes critical of others, but is realizing that such criticism is all projection of something in herself she has not yet accepted. She is part of a large family, but is striving to become more independent and think for herself.

She is attuned to nature spirits and knows when a plant needs nourishment or water. She has many plants at home and makes a large garden in the summer months. She is studying biology and botany, and can remember the Latin names for just about any species. She remembers people's names and has classification systems in her mind about rocks, plants, animals and people.

Ramon

is a wrestler, cook and filmmaker. He wants to communicate about Latino concerns in the United States and has travelled in wrestling matches to both South America and Europe. Ramon knows what he wants in his films. He direct the crew with kindness and yet is very calculating, for he knows his scripts meticulously. Within the rigid framework of the script and scenes, he is incredibly spontaneous. He has actors do impulsive things and keeps the cameras running beyond specific scenes. He does a lot of the editing himself, for some of the emotional content of the spontaneous shots are retained and some of the calculated scenes are edited out. He wants to show the authenticity of his people.

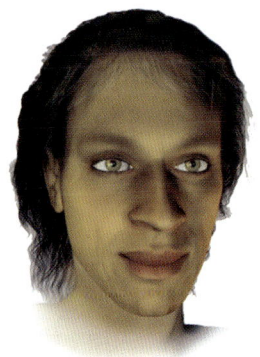

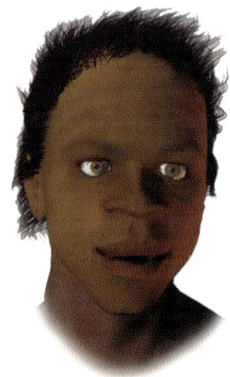

The Loop or Torus psychic attractor assists in assimilating impressions or food. It calls forth purity of motive, within psyche and body. Use this psychic attractor to hear feedback from your environment or from others and to give feedback. This means honest observation and communication.

THE COLUMN—tone of F#, create connection

The Column is the attractor of balance and extension from a balance point. The Column is vertical, meaning an axis in relation to gravity. This axis attractor is also tension between poles. The connection made by an axis may also be between cathode and anode where the poles have opposite charges.

The column attractor is opposite, in zodiacal wheel, to the point attractor *to create codes*. This attractor may also be a tension of strings or bow string. Its potential is not directly from Prime Source, but is a polarity potential. It relates to a pendulum swing without resistance.

In psychology, the axis or Column attractor is a tension between self-image and society or between soul and personality. Perception and expression seek to connect in harmony. In the body, this psychic attractor is represented by the spine, good posture, and standing up for oneself. Bending forward or being humped is overprotection of soul; bending back is overprotection of the personality. To keep balance is a natural curvature of an erect spine. Spirit pulls one up. Matter pulls one down. Creating connection is uniting spirit and matter. Plants do this between light and darkness, and levity and gravity.

Symbols: Axis, Pole, Tree, May pole,

Dolores

finds it easy to harmonize with all kinds of people. She has a lot of poise and if someone tries to overpower her, she will hesitate, but then speak her mind plainly. She connects easily with others and with Nature and tends to be a mediating influence when others have conflicts.

She obtained a law degree, but after practising a year, she decided to use her gifts in social work and community mediation. She functions best when in relation to people in direct contact rather than in public courts.

Horus

is a brilliant lawyer, whose cause has been to help refugees and foreign people in the United States. His father is from India and his mother is a New York owner of a retail store. Horus combines the soft and profoundly aware spirituality of his father and the practical sense of his mother. He enjoys equitable games—whether it be tennis or ping pong, but his purpose is focussed on administering people of diverse races and traits to come into greater cooperation.

Horus has a strong sense of fairness and though it is hard sometimes for him to make decisions, they are almost always in balance.

Visualize this psychic attractor in your spine when you need to stand up to someone or speak your truth in a balanced way. Use the column or axis to bring about a connection between two disparate tendencies—in yourself or in others.

THE WAVE—tone of G, maintain flow

The Wave attractor is an energy mover, and transmitter. Duplication of a wave in time is maintenance. The electromagnetic spectrum (as codes) is carried by waves of various frequencies—all of which are energy flow. The Wave attractor contains three parameters of information, while being itself energy: wavelength, frequency, and amplitude. These are experienced as pitch, octave and loudness in sound.

How does energy flow and keep flowing? Amplifying or cancelling are its rules of opposites, and waving in continuity are its rules of similars. The wave is related to time's arrow. Thermodynamically, time goes only one direction: entropic (running down). But negentropic is maintaining flow in anti-time. Thus the wave attractor is a cycle and can be seen either as a wave or as a cycle. Potential to matter is entropic and matter to potential is negentropic. Life and consciousness are negentropic. Through consciousness we create potential, which maintains the flow of energy creating matter. Animals maintain flow through internal vital energy, expressed as movement.

The Wave attractor in psychology is in how consciousness uses time. One can do more in less time through prioritizing and getting to the essence. Anti-aging is using consciousness in the eternal now. High amplitude is a vertical wave where one's intensity of consciousness does more in less time. Long wavelengths endure, but do little. Short wavelengths burn out, but do a lot in a short time. Reciprocity is a give and take of energy by means of a wave sent back and forth. The containment field sends the wave back to the sender. Here is a psychology of transmitting and receiving, giving and taking.

Symbols: T'ai Chi

Ratta

is highly sexual, but she is also highly discerning and therefore sublimates much of her sexual energy into artistic expression. She is studying to be a psychiatrist, for she has a hypnotizing effect on people, usually in very beneficial ways. She is very independent and so it is difficult for her to do formal study in an institution, but she has chosen to have credentials. Then she will be able to use her gifts directly in healing and art. She also facilitates art therapy.

David

is extremely intense and he uses his excess energy in sports—especially swimming. Competitive sports he loves as a game, but does not take them seriously enough to "win." He has become emotionally stable through many relationships. Because he is sexually attractive to women, he has had a hard time prioritizing his relationships, but he is opening his heart more and more, becoming compassionate as well as passionate.

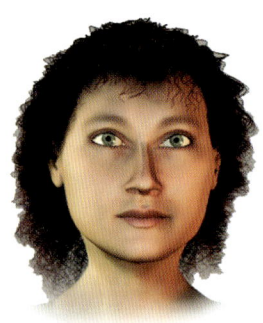

Use the Wave psychic attractor to be consistent in your energy flow and emotional stability. If you have a message to send someone, use this attractor for transmission. You can use shortwaves or long waves depending on the intensity and duration of your concern. This psychic attractor can discharge excess psychic energy and recharge so that you can more clearly live your soul purpose.

THE DIAMOND—tone of Ab, transform Codes

The Diamond psychic attractor reveals recursive nesting and perfect symmetry. It returns codes to their source after transformation. The diamond is the attractor of self-similars in diverse scales. It is highly holographic through difference of scale and nesting of patterns, one inside the other. Every part is a whole and a mirror of the Whole. This holographic attractor returns the codes to their source by transforming in dimensions, scale and symmetry. This is a kind of implosion, a black hole or place where light vanishes in three dimensions and reappears in higher dimensions. The Diamond psychic attractor is a refracted hologram of self within Prime Source.

Psychologically this attractor may be death and rebirth, a release of identity of personality, and a realization of soul or spirit. It is an offering to God one's treasury of experience and wisdom.

Symbols: Nested Boxes, Diamond, Mirror, Pearls or Gems of wisdom.

Humphrey

is very astute at everything he does, but his main quality is that he simply is. He doesn't take any of his roles too seriously and yet fulfills them meticulously. He is a writer of fiction, and his stories are like Chinese boxes, with one story inside another. His detail for character reflects in the stories on many levels and reveal the inner nature of parallel characters. He lives in a state of paradox, for he knows that the three-dimensional world is a display of consciousness. He is a teacher of sorts, for everywhere he goes, he offers subtle insights to people he meets.

He rides horses on his ranch for relaxation and inspiration. They are his closest friends as they are so authentic. Humphrey looks for authenticity everywhere.

Clare

has undergone many transformations in one lifetime. Some may say she has lived many lives in this one. She has been mosaic artist, executive, wife, jeweler, and teacher. Her passion is to understand the relationships of matter to life, and of life to spirit and consciousness. She has searched through myths of all ages and cultures to find the patterns of spiritual traditions. Though she has the capability of a scholar, she prefers to communicate in direct, simple words, metaphors, and symbols.

Presently, she designs logos for companies and corporations for she penetrates into the intent of the organization and comes up with brilliant images that represent it. She is uncompromising in her audacity, and won't do logos for institutions that do not have, in her estimation, worthy purposes.

Use the diamond psychic attractor when you are absolutely needing to be one with spirit. Visualize the diamond all around you and within you as a purified spiritual mirroring of your essence. Face all your "shadows" and be willing to live in absolute truth and love. Holding this intent with infinite intensity and compassion for yourself, enables you to move in many dimensions of consciousness.

THE SPHERE—tone of A, create substance

To create substance is to create effects, that is, to manifest. This is a one-point attractor that is fixed and accumulative around a center. The Sphere attractor is protective and material while also being creative. In ecology, this attractor is a habitat. For plants it is the roots and also cell walls. This attractor is nuclear, not in the seed sense of creating codes, but as an attractor at the center of accumulated density. This attractor is used in protein synthesis in cells, compaction of rocks in planets, technology and agriculture in culture. For animals, this attractor is the dark, safe hollow of a nest, cave, or hole—a place to rest and recuperate as well as to bear offspring.

For humans, the Sphere attractor is the recapitulation of the animal development in an embryo. On the atomic level, this attractor is the strong nuclear force. Among grids, it is the crystal as a manifest grid. On the subatomic level, this attractor is the gluons and quarks. Here is the deep resistance of matter returning to the One.

Psychologically, this attractor relates to the groupie, the one who needs to be clustered around a central idea or person—an attractor that holds a fixed idea. Or it may be a tendency to protect oneself and concerns with security and insurance. It is a creative center of many products, and substances.

Symbols: Close-pack Spheres, Flower of Life.

Shobak Shu

is part Amerindian and part Mongolian and brings a profound shamanic influence among his people. He is a natural healer for he intuitively understands all stages of human growth within animal life.

He protects the animals in specific areas and travels back and forth between Mongolia and the United States where he resides with the Hopi. His prime interest is in protecting the traditional wisdom of "indigenous" peoples. He has been to New Zealand and also met with the Maori leaders and is finding the threads of common wisdom. Shobak Shu is highly creative and shares his crafts of pottery and basket-weaving with people everywhere there is interest.

Janet

is a protector of people's and animal's rights. She works as a volunteer at several community organizations and works as assistant to a CEO for the Protection of Animals Institute.

Her inner nature is very alert, sensitive, and aware. She has difficulty with people who are callous, and yet she does not press or push anyone. Her heart is most adoring of animals, as they are always true to themselves.

She is excellent at organization, but doesn't like to deal with too many details, although she has to at times. She stands up for her friends and often is the glue for her family.

She does hiking and even mountain climbing in her spare time, and in winter, she loves skiing.

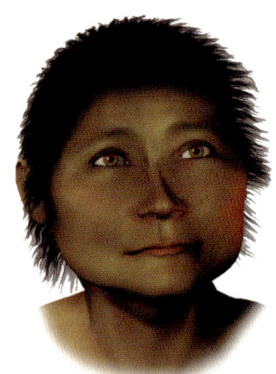  

Use the Sphere psychic attractor for protection. Visualize it all around your auric field as a sphere of blue light. This psychic attractor is beneficial when you need rest and recuperation. Imagine it like a dark cave or spherical room. Visualize the blue sphere is a container for creating and manifesting some material idea you have.

THE GRID—tone of Bb, maintain connection

This attractor is a network, a Grid that interconnects. In our day, the world wide web is the supreme example. There is no clustering here, but just the opposite: an expansive network with no central hub.

According to the principle of equipartition, if heat energy were applied as a specific vibration in a lattice of metal, you would think the energy might distribute out in the lattice, but it doesn't. It bunches into nodes and tones. It becomes a soliton. It is like the self-focusing of giant waves in the ocean and the meeting of currents in tidal waves. The lattice is fixed; whereas the waves are moving.

In cells, the Grid attractor appears in aspects of the endoplasmic reticulum, and in planets, it is found in faults and fissures. In culture the grid functions in mathematics and education. The grids of space function through galaxies and stars, and in ecology, there are grid ley lines and ancestral song lines. The analogical mind is an invisible grid in humans; whereas in the subatomic realm, grids relate to space-time curvature. In animals, grids are both memory and ecological matrices, and on the atomic level, grids are found especially in ionic bonds of crystal lattices.

Symbols: Lattices, Geodesic Structures

Joe

is both a basketball player and computer design specialist. Everyone tends to like him as he is loving and full of humour. When young, he built radios and also weather instruments. He is fascinated with anything that communicates by waves through the air. He grew up in the United States, but is interested in going to Africa to relate to his racial roots, someday.

Joe uses technology as a means for inter-communication. His greatest happiness is often when telepathy precedes technology. He often receives emails after having thought of someone.

In basketball, he is very aware of the opposing team and plays aware of his own team's gifts and drawbacks in relation to the opponents.

Wadabu

is a black African with a German father! She was born in South Africa and is interested in politics insofar as it can assist with equality among races. She speaks the Zulu language, good English, and German. She is setting up an international hub for racial problems throughout the world. She and her partner train teams of people to train others in communication, mediation, and games. The games are different ways that peoples test and amuse themselves with relaxation. When the games are played, opposing sides begin to appreciate the other side a little more.

Every applicant must speak at least two languages and be willing to travel to countries with racial conflict. Wadabu is very compassionate and has a sense of humour.

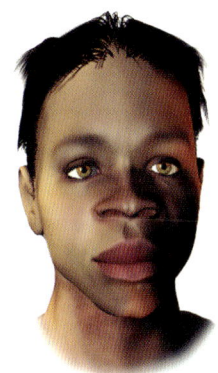

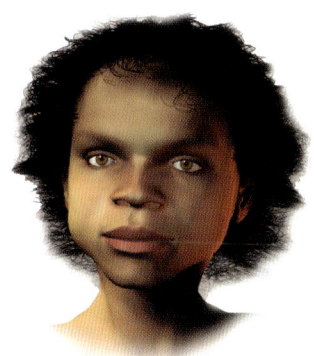

Use the Grid psychic attractor to communicate at a distance and even anticipate what someone is doing or thinking. It is beneficial in prayers for friends, peoples across the globe or those who are needy. Use it to both receive and send messages and also to keep your computer in good working order.

THE UNPREDICTABLE—tone of B, transform flow

The Unpredictable attractor is excellent for dissolving past, unwanted experiences. This attractor is represented in vastness, wholeness and the void. A patternless pattern appears within the unknowable. The attractor of Unpredictability is of broken symmetries and so-called "randomness." It might appear as layers of shifting dimensional orders that appear chaotic, sometimes called "laminar." The Unpredictable attractor has analogy to the homogeneity of space with no symmetry.

In cells, you can observe it in cytomplasmic streaming; and in planets in the molten core and deep seas. It is the soil and decay within soil for plants and in the atomic realm it relates to the weak nuclear force of radioactive decay. For stars, it is the quantum flux of zero-point energy, and for galaxies, the Unpredictable attractor is found in interstellar gas and dust. In ecology in general, this attractor relates to recycling through decomposition, and among grids, it is irregular. The personality of the Unpredictable is wandering, uncertain, unreliable.

You can find this Unpredictable attractor in the death-rites of animals and the collective unconscious of culture. Among humans it is either the shadows of the unconscious or in mystic states where there is a dissolution of ego.

Symbols: Flotsom and Jetsam, Clouds

Ingalook

is extremely sensitive to wildlife of all kinds. He loves dolphins, elk, and wild birds as well as insects and all kinds of plant life. He grew up in Alaska and is familiar with oil spills and environmental devastation and is working with environmental groups to change the trend of destruction to wildlife.

Though he takes an active part in environmental groups, he is finding that his prayers and shamanic drumming are assisting as much or more than management. He is tuned in to the devas and nature spirits, and works with them to harmonize human with plant and animal life. He is a very happy man by nature, but when sorrow penetrates, it is very deep.

Radha

has a very poetic soul and is very deep. She has some difficulty in being accepted fully, as she is so deeply inward and also seems unreliable to other people. In truth, she is exploring her inner life, and although she has studied psychology, she finds that it is not intuitive enough for her to use.

She prefers poetry, painting, singing, and cooking. Whenever she gets social, she likes to cook for people and has many wild food and natural recipes she uses. She is very tuned into the essential Void within and behind everything. Whenever she feels conflict or criticism, she simply goes into the Void and finds solace. She is somewhat moody, but is learning how to release psychological ups and downs.

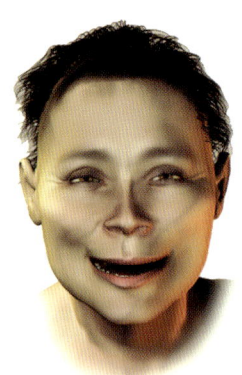  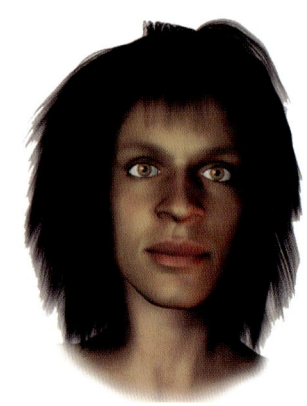

Use the Unpredictable psychic attractor to dissolve old wounds, frustrations, and conflicts. The attitude is one of surrender to the will of the One and work for the good of the whole. Use this form in visualizations within any area of the body that needs dissolution of blockages. Surround yourself with a floating, unpredictable, mysterious cloud and accept everything as it is.

Exercise

Meditate on your body a while, feeling your energy body. Visualize your chakras. Then, using the *Co-Creation Code Deck*, pick seven cards with the intention of having insight into and healing any imbalances in your chakras. **Each card does not represent a specific chakra.** Rather, you are asking your guides to reveal to you where there are any imbalances in your chakras, by having one or more cards falling into a given chakra. Use the chart below to find out which chakras need balancing.

Example: If you pick any of the cards represented in the row of the base chakra (bottom row) then there is some imbalance there. If you have no cards for the base chakra, then there is balance there right now. You may have two, three or four cards in a given chakra and none in others. Read the sections for each card from the *Co-Creation Code Deck* book and interpret for your given chakra.

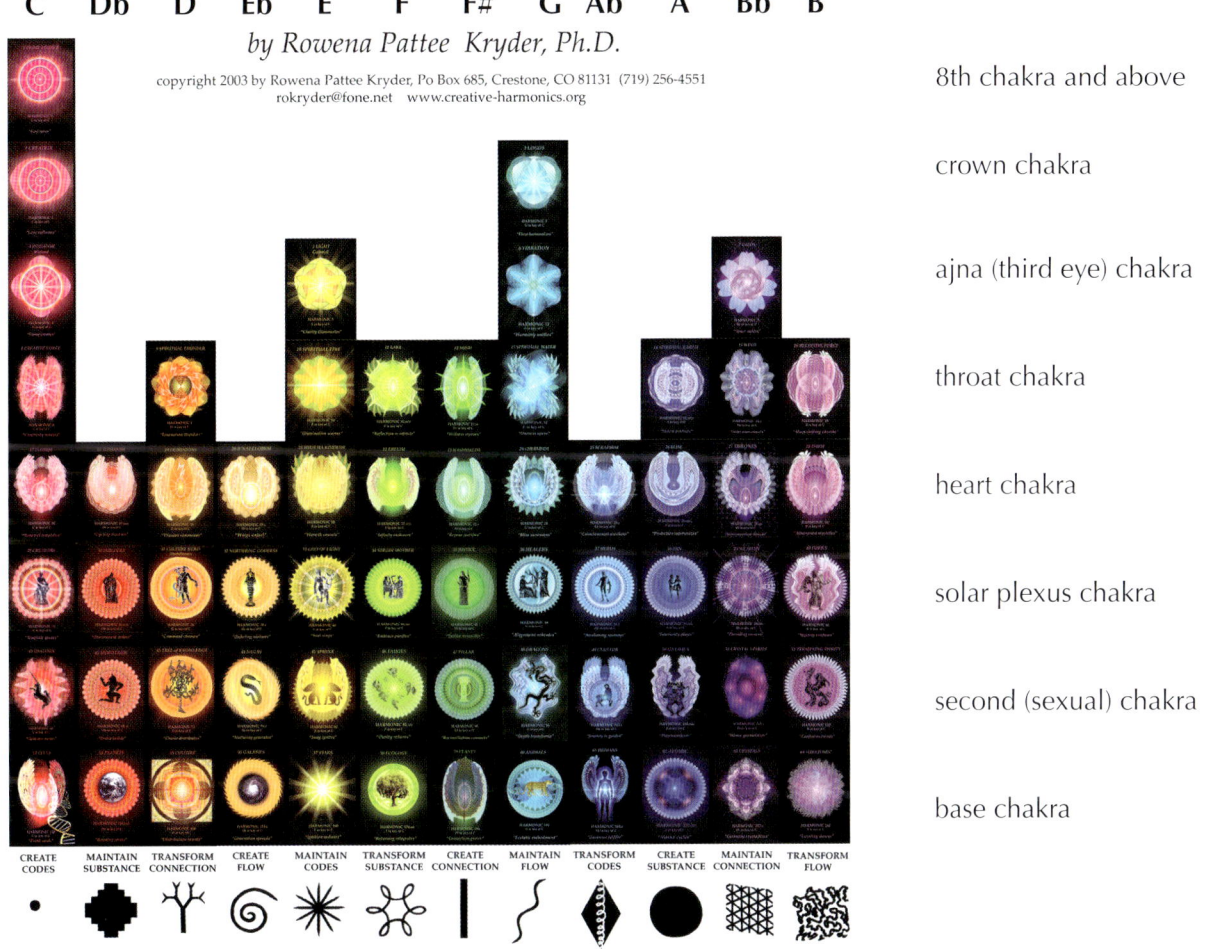

Now visualize the **form** of the psychic attractor in the relevant chakra of your energy body, relating to the cards you picked. You may have no psychic attractors in some chakras and two, three or four in one chakra. When you have psychic attractors in a given chakra, it means that chakra needs balancing—either activation or release. Chakras that have no psychic attractors in them are in balance at the moment.

If you do this exercise once a week, or even more often, you will find different chakras need balancing. This is because you are activating and releasing in layers of subtle energy.

The important thing is to visualize the psychic attractor in the chakra and see how they behave as energy forms and color. You may have various shapes of spirals, for example, or large or small and highly active or subtly active. Make note of these qualities and perhaps draw them. When you have more than one psychic attractor in a given chakra, see how the forms interact within your energy field. Remain receptive and open to insights and let the psychic attractors balance your chakras.

Chapter Five:
INNER LANDSCAPES AND THE INNER CHILD

Each of our characters has an inner life just as you do. All of them are here introduced as youths, because the inner life reflects the youthful mind-heart. You might regard it as the inner child. The inner child is that aspect of ourselves that has a soul purpose, is impulsive, carries old wounds, and yet is innocent, and dreams. The inner child is seeking contact with the world and yet wants to be recognized as he/she is.

Sometimes dreams and visions reveal landscapes that are also filled with symbols. See if you can discern more about yourself through the twenty-four characters by looking at the male and female complementarity of the twelve archetypes. See if you identify with one or more of the characters. Make notes. Observe the pattern of each psychic attractor made into a tile and make notes about which ones you are attracted to and which ones you are even repelled by, or are indifferent to.

Exercise

These patterns are but a few among many possibilities of each psychic attractor. You might draw your own. For example, the spiral can be single, double, triple, or more. It may be in wide arcs of spirals or very narrow and almost uniform as on a CD disk. A branch might be a single branch, or multiples. Its branches might be straight or curved, with many branches coming from each node or only two. The radial might be as simple as a cross or as complex as having millions of radial lines like a star. The wave might be just a little swell or a high, tumultuous, many frequenced wave. Use your imagination and feeling on this exercise.

Now read the simple statements of each one in the following pages. Which qualities do you need now? Which qualities do you already have? What qualities do you aspire to? Then, if you know your astrology chart, you can make correlations with the zodiacal signs. You at least likely know when you were born, and although exact relations to zodiacal signs may vary from year to year, you can, in general, use the following birth dates:

December 22 to January 21 = Capricorn
January 22 to February 21 = Aquarius
February 22 to March 21 = Pisces
March 22 to April 21 = Aries
April 22 to May 21 = Taurus
May 22 to June 21 = Gemini
June 22 to July 21 = Cancer
July 22 to August 21 = Leo
August 22 to September 21 = Virgo
September 22 to October 21 = Libra
October 22 to November 21 = Scorpio
November 22 to December 21 = Sagittarius
(For exact dates of transition between zodiacal signs each year, consult a calendar or ephemeris.)

I am relating zodiacal signs simply because these are cosmic processes of time that are archetypal or symbolic in nature. Therefore, the symbolism is part of the pattern I'm intending for you, the reader to resonate to, and make part of your power and understanding.

Ariel

I am reaching for Source!

♈ Aries, tone of C, create codes

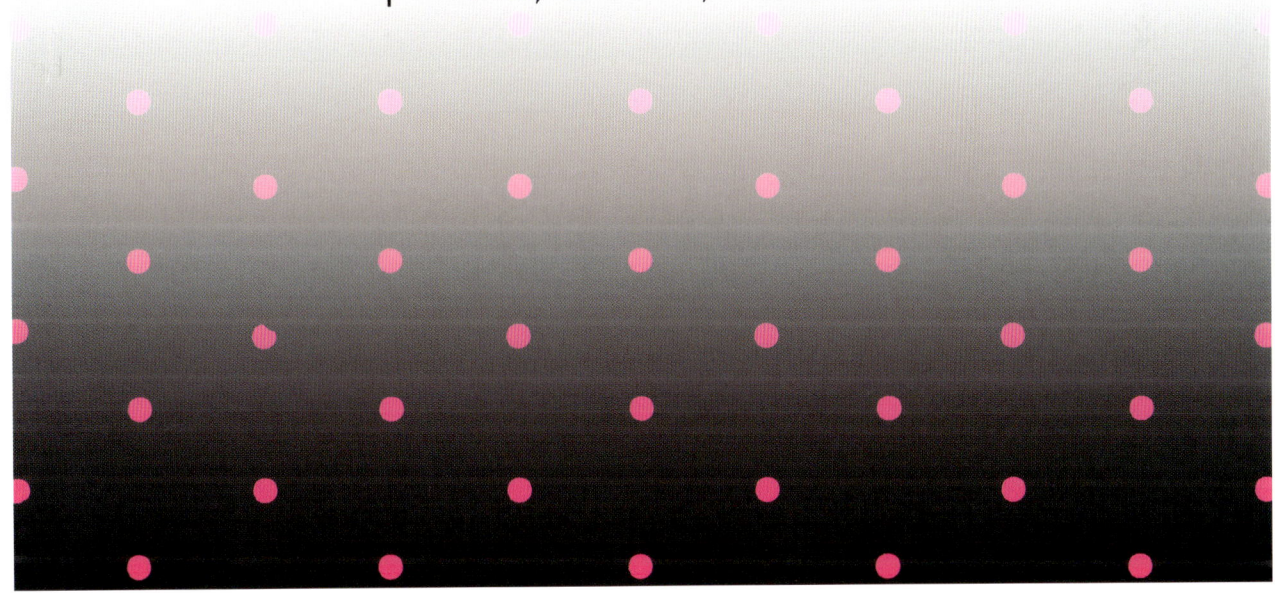

Shawn

Frank

I am unswerving in my committment to life

♉ **Taurus—tone of Db, maintain substance**

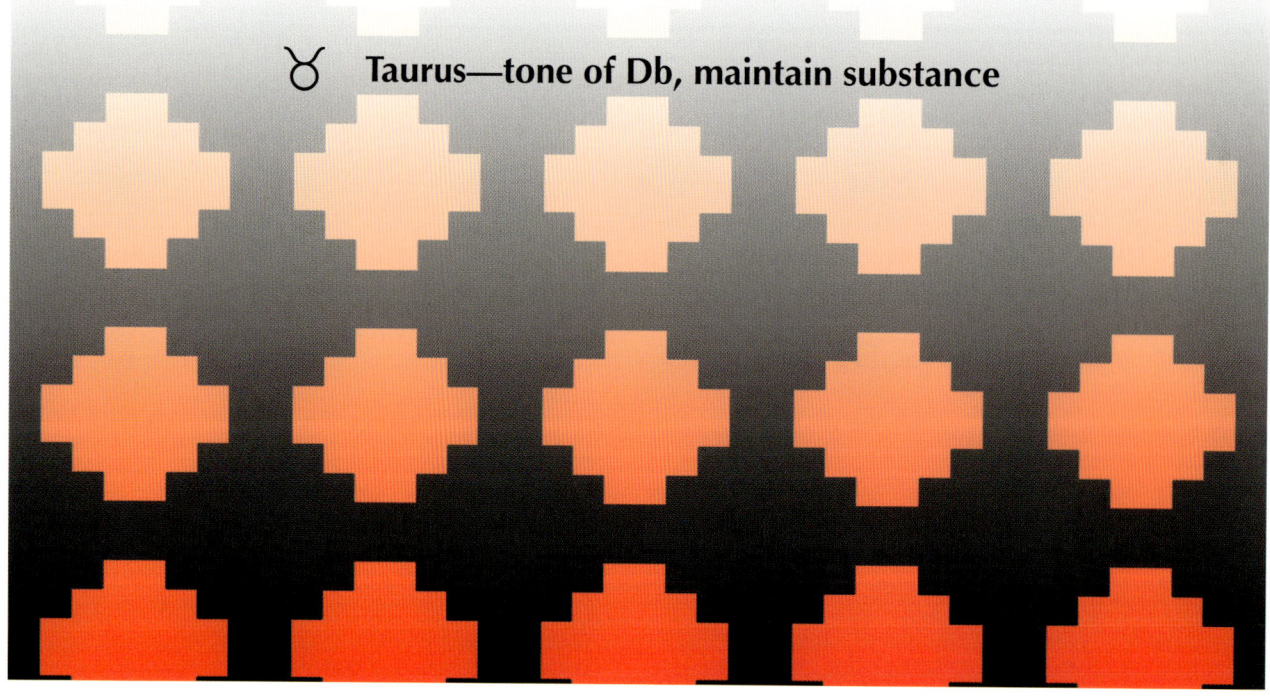

Elizabeth

Karen

I contemplate the diversity of life

Ⅱ   Gemini—tone of D, transform connection

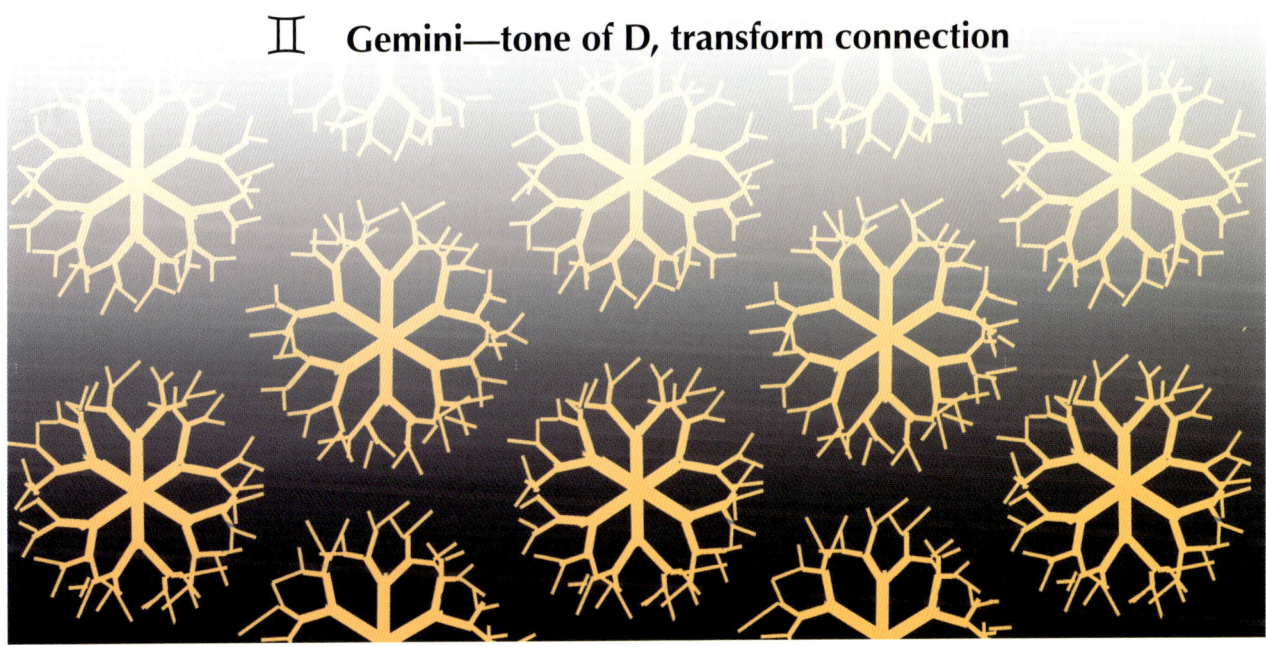

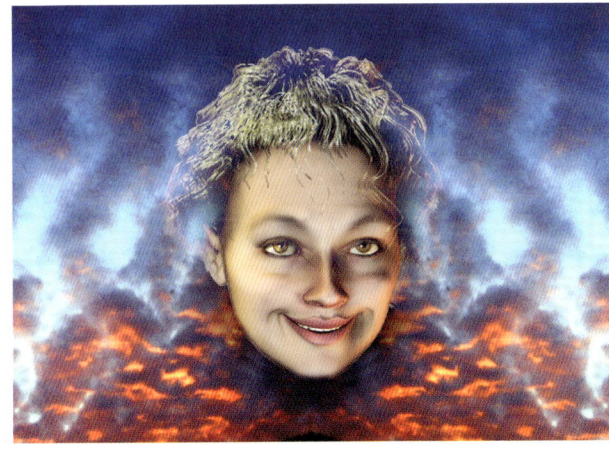

Morgan

Ricardo

I spin and dance with ecstasy

☋ **Cancer—tone of Eb, create energy flow**

Jennifer

Serafina

I reveal the power of my heart

♌ Leo—tone of E, maintain codes

Francis

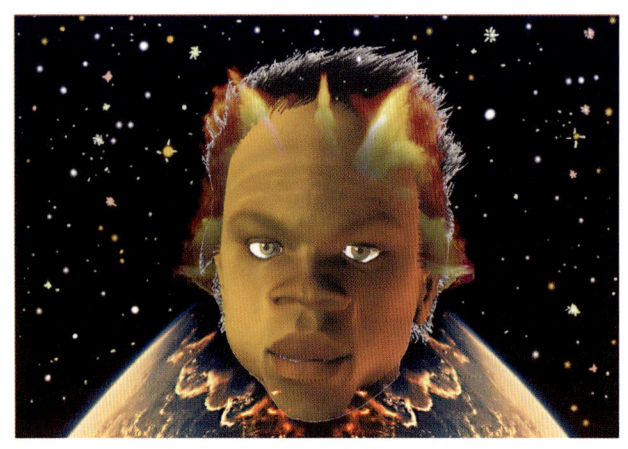

Ramon

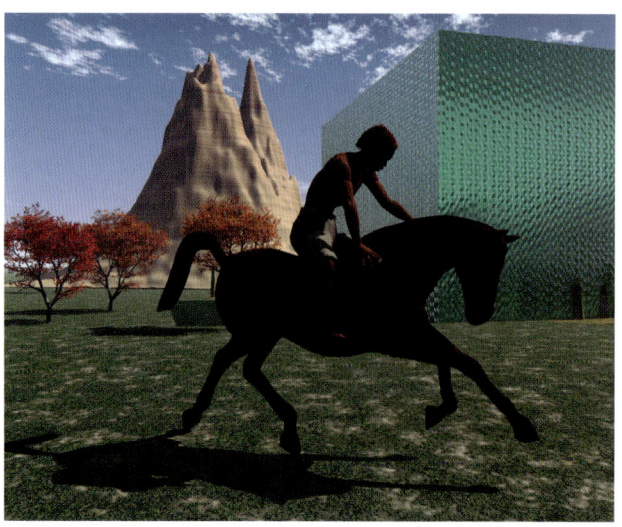

I discern true and false in practical ways

 Virgo—tone of F, transform substance

Francesca

Horus

I see the relations of high and low

♎ **Libra—tone of F#, create connection**

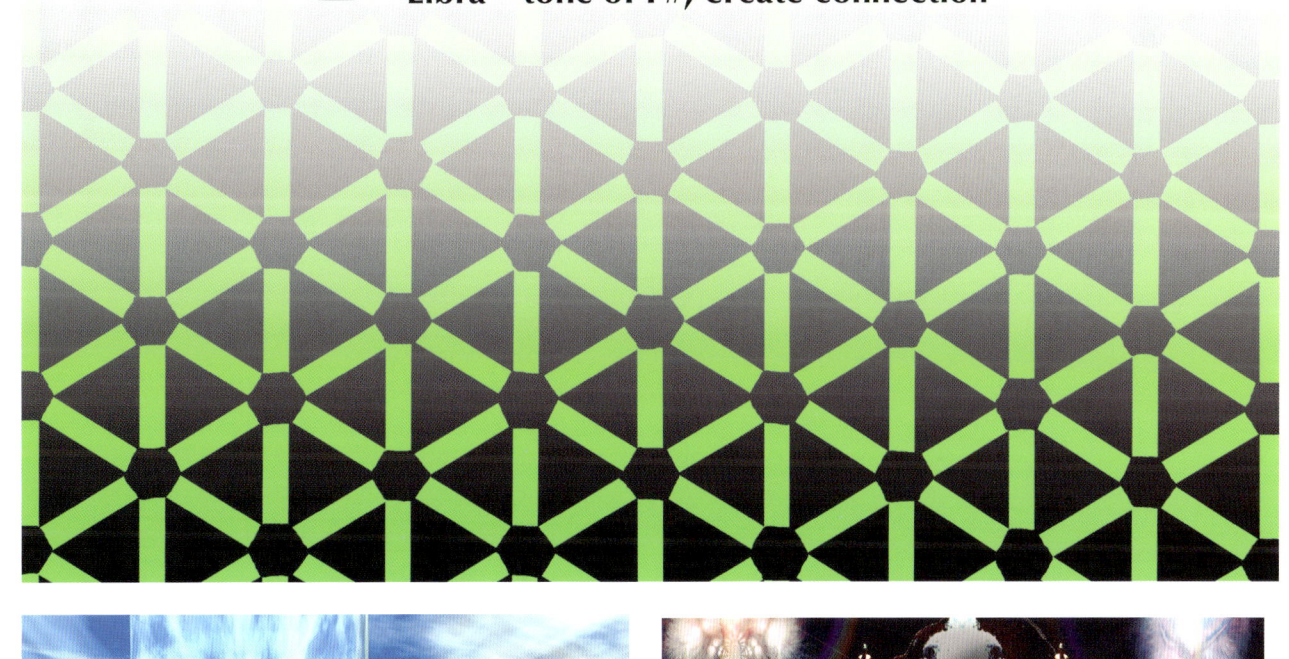

Dolores

Ratta

I interact with the wildest of things

♏ **Scorpio—tone of G, maintain energy flow**

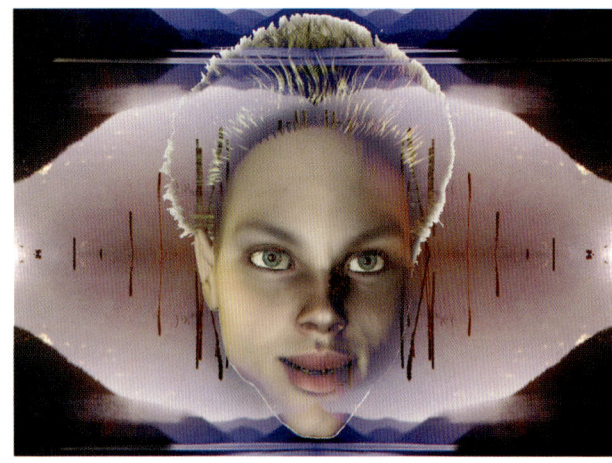

David

Humphrey

My reflections take me straight to where I am

♐ **Sagittarius—tone of Ab, transform codes**

Clare

Shobak Shu

I love to contemplate deep places of beauty

 Capricorn—tone of A, create substance

Janet

Wabadu

There is no limit to the miracles of life

♒ **Aquarius, tone of Bb, maintain connection**

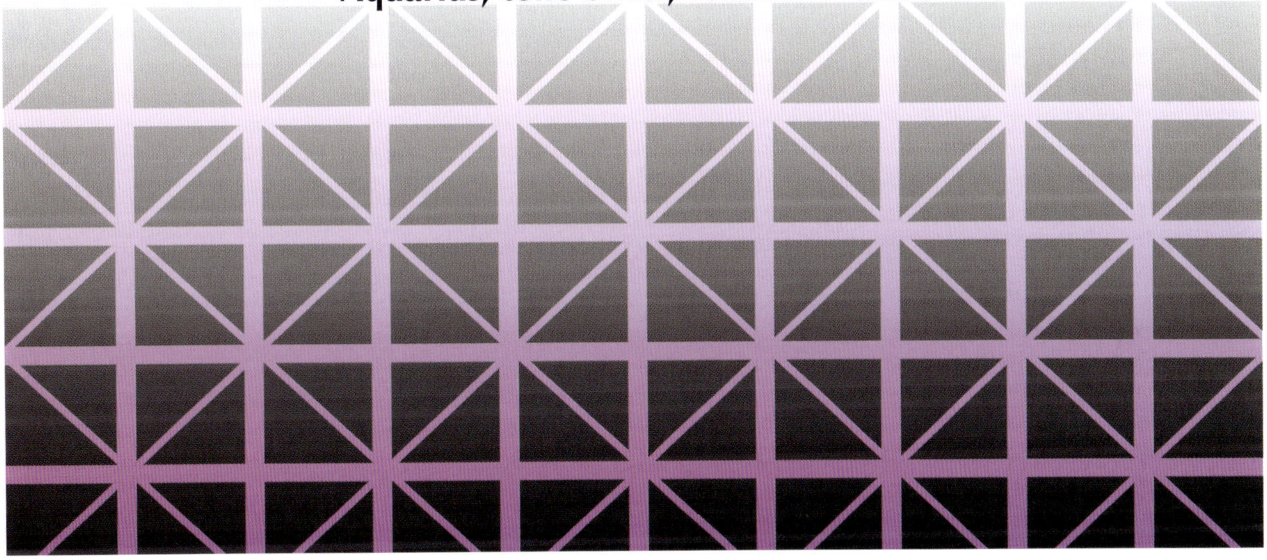

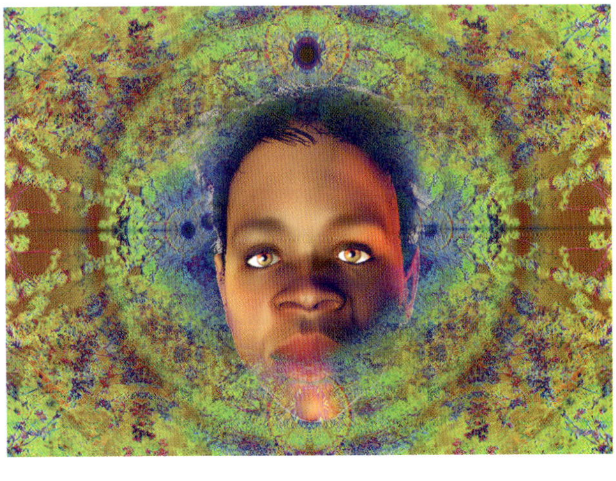

Joe

Radha

I flow wherever the dance of life takes me

 **Pisces—tone of B, transform energy flow**

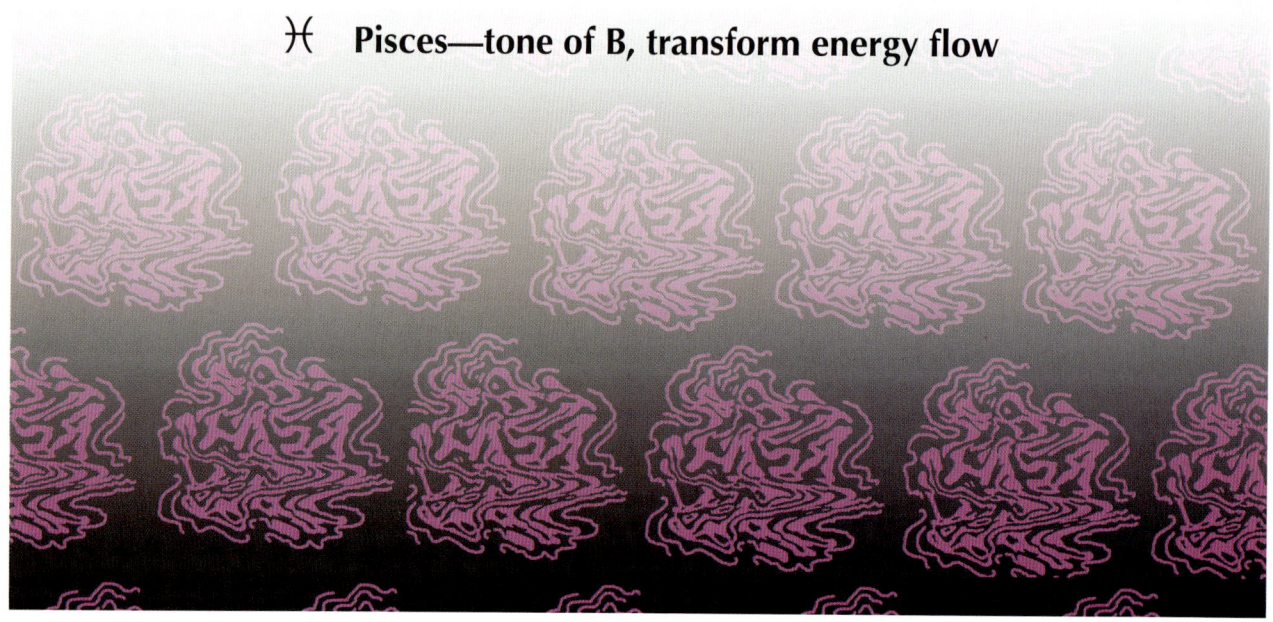

Ingalook

Part Two
ROBES OF LIGHT

In the following sections, you will have an opportunity to find which of the twelve archetypes are most relevant to your own soul purpose. The robes are patterns of form and color that speak to the tribal instincts and to the soul. The robes are aspects of auric fields and might be seen as virtual or light-body robes. If you allow it, your inner life will resonate to one or more of the robe patterns. This may be an indicator of your soul resonance. Throughout this book, I will give indicators that might assist you in finding your soul purpose and your soul tribe. Here tribe does not mean something clannish or elitist in anyway, nor does it refer to simply conditioned tribal habits, but a deep inner well-spring or divine source for you to draw upon in the unfoldment of your life. The robes stand for your light body. There are nine stages of initiation in the life-process of integrating all nine light bodies. This book is an outline for these initiations. For more in-depth work, look under workshops on the web: **www.creative-harmonics.org.**

First Initiation—Ren: Find your spiritual name from the resonance of sounds. This is your basic constitutional archetype. It likely consists of several of the colors, patterns, and chakras.

Second Initiation—Khat: Your Khat is a template for your physical body and can be accessed by scanning your whole body with your consciousness, from head to toe and from toe to head. Vipassana meditation is a good practise for this.

Third Initiation—Ka: Discover a series of patterns and colors that resonate with your subconscious. Harmonics and sacred geometry are two sense modalities of one universal language. Find out what musical intervals, keynotes, and geometric patterns resonate most to your Ka light body.

Fourth Initiation—Khaibit: Your Khaibit is your unconscious. How can you be conscious of your unconscious? The first step is having the intention to open to your shadows, those experiences you once denied and did not want to deal with. Now, as you open to past pain, trauma, and secrets, you will have the opportunity to meet your Khaibit, who is really simply holding the treasury of your energy field for when you want to claim it.

Fifth Initiation—Ab: Your conscience enables you not only to face what you once denied, but to take responsibility for it and to forgive yourself and others involved. When you know your Ab intimately, you can see and feel from another's point of view and know the goodness for the whole.

Sixth Initiation—Ba: To know your soul is to know your purpose in life. The Ba is reflected in the Ab (conscience), so for your soul to speak to you or for you to feel its presence, you must have a clear conscience.

Seventh Initiation—Sekhem: The Sekhem is the life force, but even more, it is kundalini energy. When the Sekhem fulfills its purpose, the kundalini energy or life-force is not dissipated through sensory pleasures, desire and fears, (the two side channels of duality), but is directed up the central, neutral channel from the base of the spine into the brain and higher chakras.

Eighth Initiation—Sahu: White magic and sacred art are activated in this stage. Chant your spiritual bodies awake, sing, dance, and create paintings that harmonize with your greatest aspirations and inspirations. Discover your deepest dreams and what your mythic reality is on the highest dimensions. All the lower bodies need to participate. This is the greatest opportunity for integration and synthesis.

Ninth Initiation—Khu: When the Khu receives the kundalini energy of the Sekhem into the head, you trust and experience complete surrender to the will of Prime Source. One has superhuman powers at this stage and thus cannot enter this initiation unless living in total unconditional love. All self-protective barriers are dissolved. This book does not give but the barest suggestions of this initiation.

Chapter Six:
USING PATTERNS OF COLOR AND FORM
How do your relate to your world?

Using the functions that bring you joy, what do you most love relating to? By Looking at the robes given on the following twelve pages, see which one attracts you most. Read the excerpt about this archetype and attempt to find your robe of greatest affinity and resonance.

This exercise is first because you already have some awareness of your soul purpose, though to become more clear on it, you will have to go through the sixth initiation.

It is not meant that you identify with a tribe or group in the outer world so much as in the inner world. Your robe of light emanates from your soul purpose. To find your soul purpose, it is necessary to release society's or other people's ideas of who you are and open up to your intrinsic sense of rightness. Go back to your childhood and see where and how your parents, peers, or siblings may have influenced you. Attempt to find your uniqueness.

What are your main functions now?

Creating codes takes focus, design and planning

Maintaining substance takes building up and protecting

Transforming connection takes choices, and branching out

Creating flow takes generating energy from spinning

Maintaining codes takes radiance and broadcasting

Transforming substance takes feedback and evaluation

Creating connection takes alignment, and bridging

Maintaining flow takes transmission, movement, and continuity

Transforming codes takes love and seeing patterns within patterns

Creating substance takes a strong center and concentric accretion

Maintaining connection takes networking and seeing relations

Transforming flow takes surrender to unpredictable surprises

Point Tribe—tone of C—create codes

If you have strong focus and concentration you likely have affinity with this tribe. Qualities are a love for information for its own sake, and ability to crack codes. People with an affinity with this tribe are often quiet, inwardly focused, but when their ideas come out they are explosive. Soul purpose is strong in the Point tribe.

Those whose soul purpose is to create codes may relate to the stars and light in general. Light frequencies are codes that are maintained throughout the universe through the radiance of stars. Nuclear burning and light radiation are the way stars create the codes of the universe.

If you love light, and color, are interested in the frequencies of atomic spectra, are a musician, interested in the qualities of different tones—harmonics, you likely also have an affinity with stars. Study x-rays, brain waves, sound and color and open your mind and heart for unique applications of color and sound in hospitals and homes. You may also be a detective or intelligence agent, love languages and be interested in crop circles.

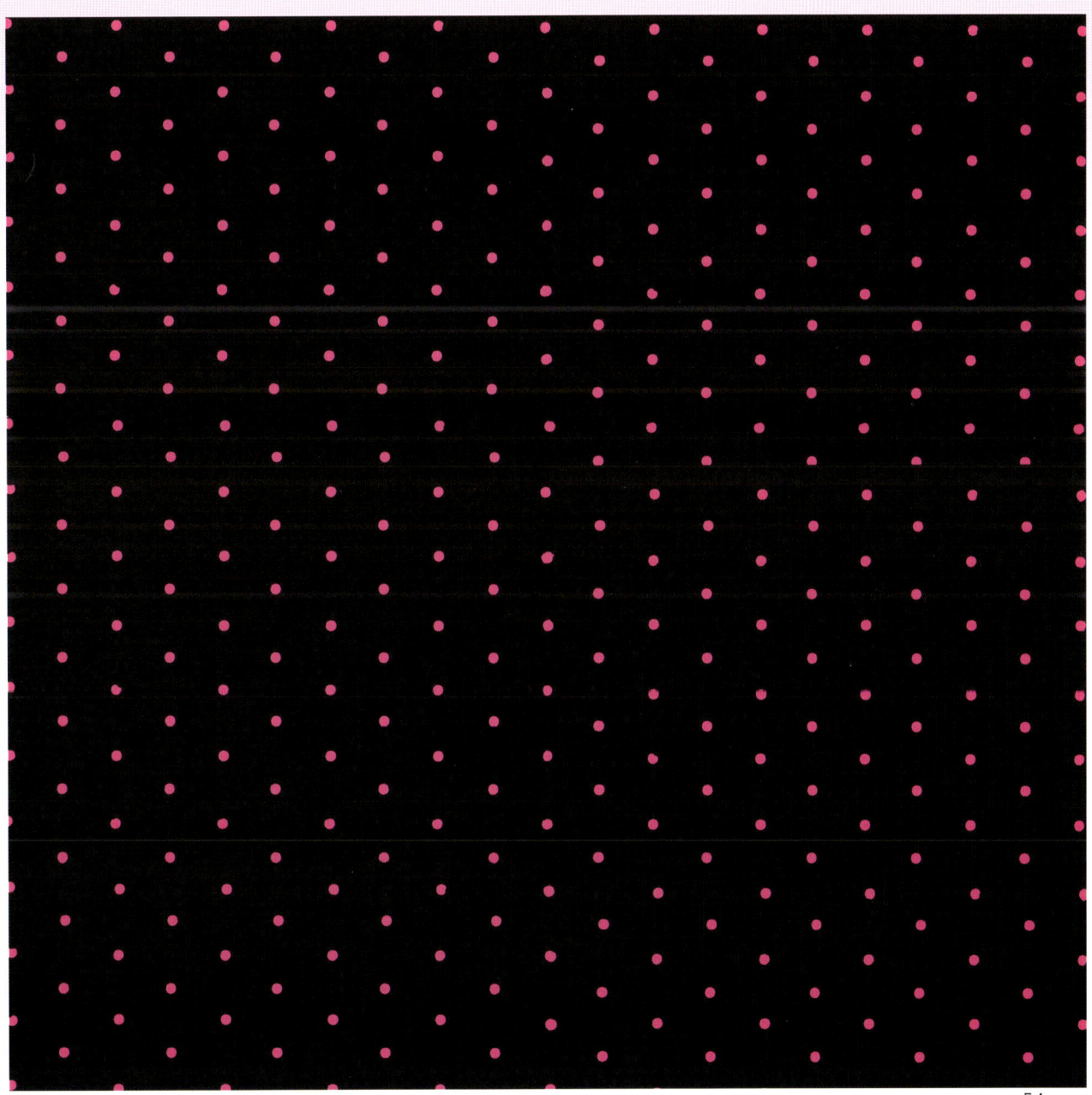

Step Tribe—tone of Db—maintain substance

If you are patient, persevering, and able to sustain long-term projects you likely have affinity with the Step tribe. Interest in money, matter, and substantial and stable situations or possessions are also qualities of those attracted to this robe.

Those whose soul purpose is to maintain substance may relate to planets. One of the main functions of planets is to build up mass, to hold its matter. Gravity is important here. If you like to build or behold monumental buildings, like the pyramids, or enjoy giant cities and massive buildings, it may be because they relate to specific functions of the planet. Megaliths and many ancient monumental buildings were located in places where mass of specific geometry was needed for maintaining the substance of the planet. Mountains serve a similar purpose and conservationists and mountain climbers relate here. There is greater pressure under mountains and pyramids than in valleys, especially if the stone is dense and/or magnetic.

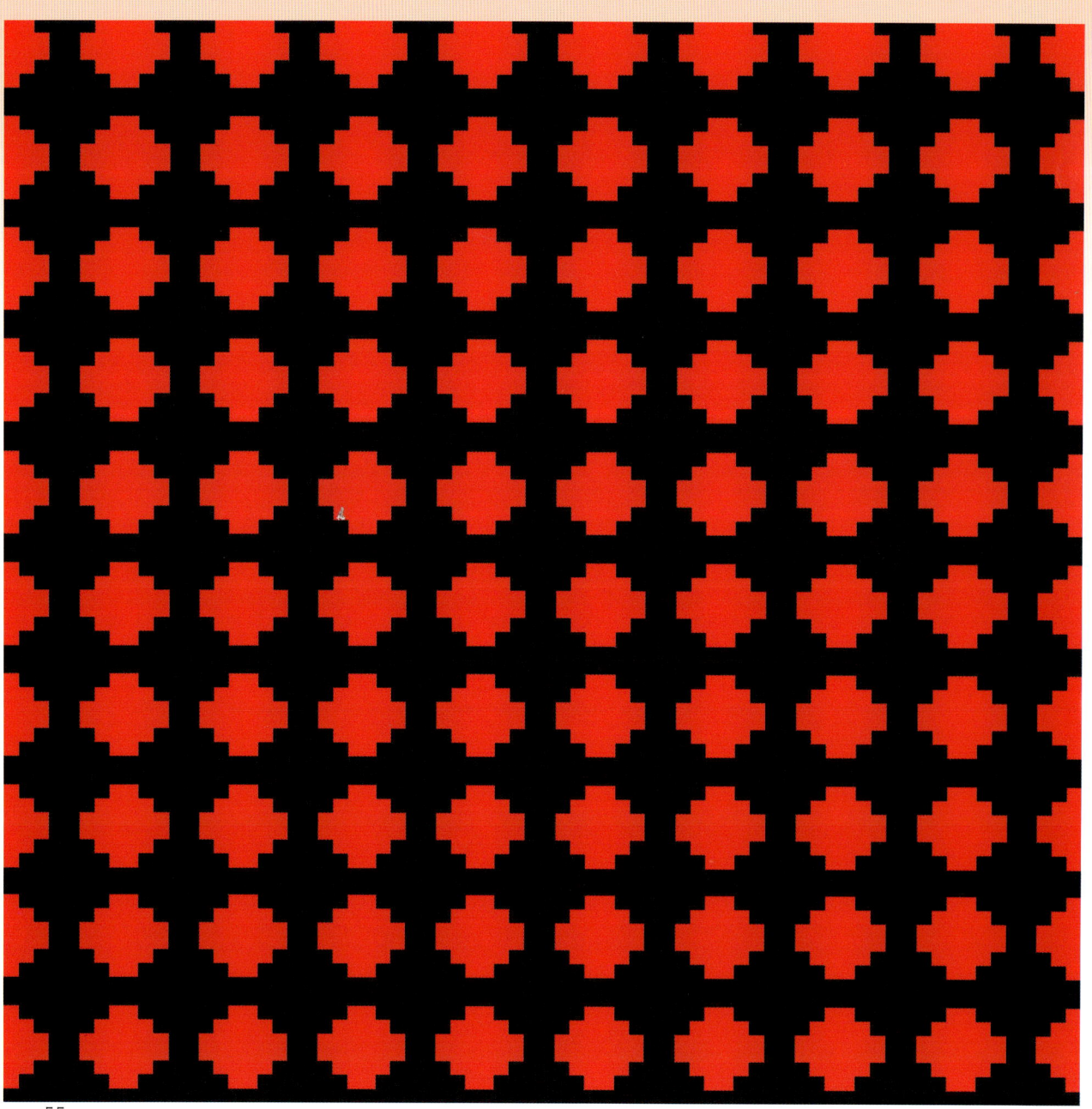

Branch Tribe—tone of D—transform connection

If you love many aspects of life, tend to get involved in numerous projects, and love to send out, share and distribute ideas, goods and projects, you likely have affinity with the Branch tribe. Branch tribe members love to branch out in all directions. They are also good communicators and often extremely intelligent, and able to manage many jobs or projects at once.

Those whose soul purpose is to transform connections may relate to cultures in general or have an interest in cross cultural vantages. One of the main functions of cultures is communications—whether through writing, radio, TV, or speaking. Communication transforms the connections between people in a given culture. Propaganda, advertising, government as well as education, distribution, and trade, are all part of this important aspect of culture distributing information. If you tend to be a cultural critic, a rebel, conflict mediator or communicator of any kind, you have some of the Branch tribe within you.

Spiral Tribe—tone of Eb—create flow

If you innately love to generate energy around your vital interests and summon other people into the momentum of energy, then you likely have affinity with the Spiral tribe. Those whose soul purpose is to create flow are innovators, not so much of ideas as of energy and enthusiasm. This robe tends to reveal vortices of energy flow both clockwise and counterclockwise. Spinning in and spinning out are balanced generators.

Those whose soul purpose is to create flow may relate to galaxies as generators of energy. Galaxies — especially those that spin and spiral, for new stars are born through this rotating motion—are giant energy generators. If you like to spin or are interested in energy generation of any kind, you have an affinity with the Spiral tribe. If you tend to generate energy flow, either with people (as a facilitator, shaman or ritualist) or with a natural energy resource—water especially—then you are an artist that creates flow.

Radial Tribe—tone of E—maintain codes

If you love to broadcast, to radiate to others, then you likely have affinity with the Radial tribe. Qualities are loving to be in the lime-light, but also generosity; questioning authority, but also leading others. If you resonate to this Robe of Light, you may also have great ability to decipher codes, then announce secrets to others. You are likely to have interest in ideas and launch them into a community.

Those, whose soul purpose is to maintain codes may relate to their cells. One of the main function of cells is to maintain codes by means of the DNA in the nucleus. Cells have all the other functions as well. If you tend to be a designer, programmer, or theorist you are operating like the DNA or chromosomes in the nucleus of a cell. This important job cannot have wobbly operators. You need to be clear and make clear programs for particular purposes. This function is not only related to cells, but to any form of code transmission, whether of light, language, or symbols.

Loop Tribe—tone of F—transform substance

Those whose soul purpose is to transform substance may relate to ecology in general. Ecology is a way of understanding the food chain essentially. It reveals the cooperative and competitive relations of living systems with the elements and time. The food chain is a kind of planetary digestive system. If you are interested in nutrition, diet or perhaps chemistry and pharmacy, you may relate to this soul purpose. The role of the human predator in the food chain is a major concern for this soul purpose.

Magicians, jewellers, and integrators of all kinds may be other expressions of transforming substance. If you like to give feedback to others and receive feedback in order to integrate and order your understanding, you likely relate to the Loop-Torus tribe.

Column Tribe—tone of F#—create connection

People whose soul purpose is to create connection are often interested in balance, uprightness, and mediation. You might be a diplomat, educator, or lawyer. Such people may be unassuming but want justice. If you love to create connections, especially between opposites or complements, you are a bridge maker. Creating connections interests inventors as well. How things and people connect is fundamental to the spaces of the universe.

Those whose soul purpose is to create connection may especially relate to plants—which create a connection between light (through photosynthesis) and gravity/darkness (through soil) by means of roots, a vertical stem and leaves.

If your tendency in conflict is to hesitate, then weigh and balance both sides of the conflict, you have traits of the Column tribe.

Wave Tribe—tone of G—maintain flow

People with affinity with the Wave tribe are intense, deep, and often sexually attractive. They may also relate to the innocence, beauty, and lively movements of animals. The wave motion is in this psychic attractor, so interest in all kinds of waves may be part of it. If you want to be a healer, facilitator, or enjoy public relations then your function may be maintaining flow. Do you like to keep energy flowing through all systems, relationships? Animals do this, for through their bodies, energy is flowing, and during courtship dances, animals are at their peak of energy flow. The sexual act is a rhythmic pump to maintain the flow of energy current through the species. This also relates to interest in conductivity and electrical current. So-called "animal magnetism" is also often an ingredient. Healing is essentially maintaining the flow of energy throughout the body.

Diamond Tribe—tone of Ab—transform codes:

Diamond tribe people can see and appreciate the relationship and hierarchy of numerous beings within a whole. Those whose soul purpose is to transform codes relate to human beings whose greater purpose is to transform all the codes we receive through the spiritual soul. The main human function is to love and to acknowledge all beings as they are. Of course we have all the other functions, but unconditional love is the key. If you tend to want to meditate, pray, or have an interest in depth psychology, your path is that of love and activation of the spiritual soul. This soul purpose, like all the transformers, involves a degree of sacrifice of the "lower" for the "higher" and a recognition of the love for Prime Source and all of creation.

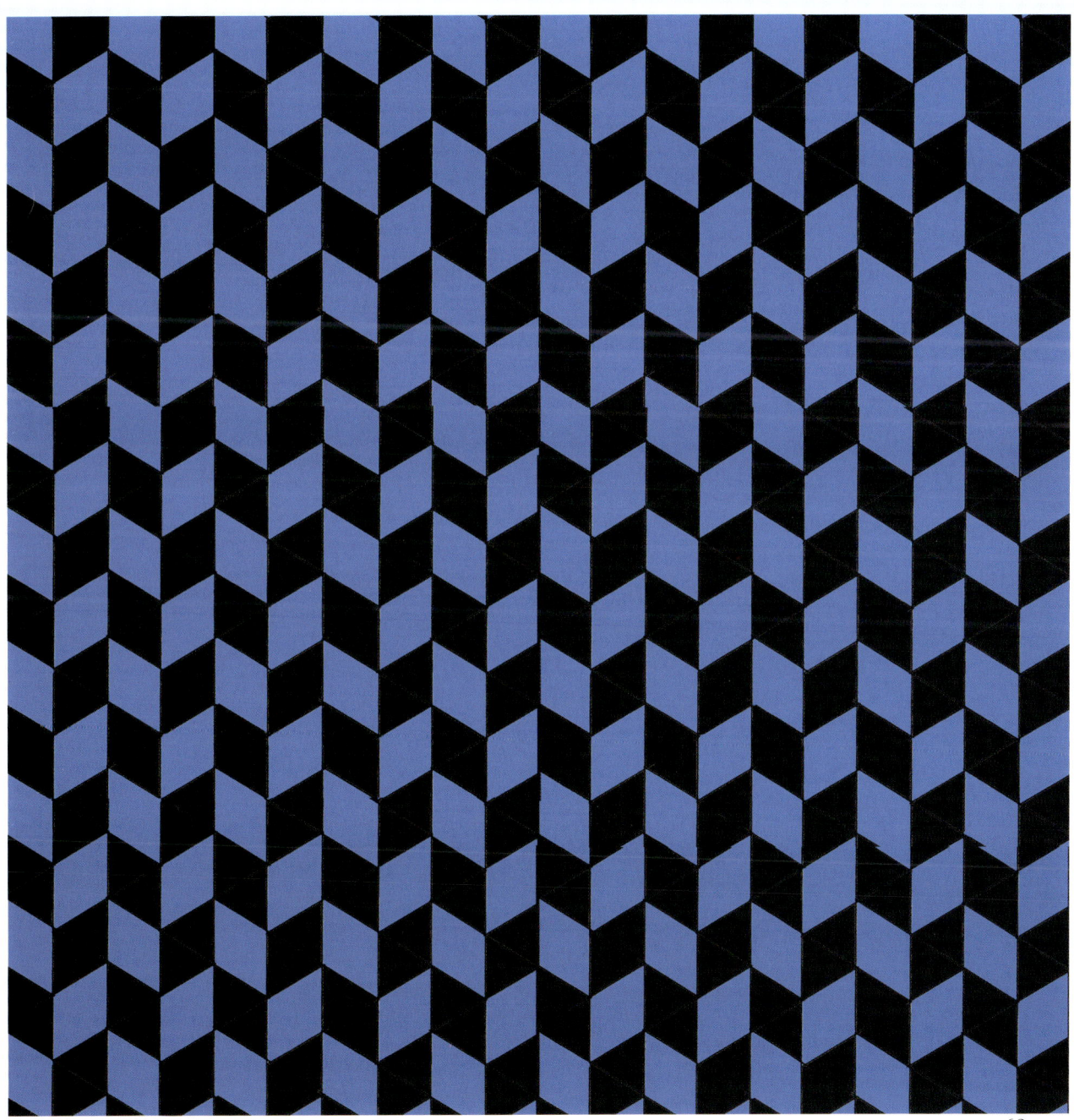

Sphere Tribe—tone of A—create substance

People with affinity with the Sphere Tribe love to create from matter, that is materials of various kinds: clay, stone, wood, brick, metal of synthetic materials. They have the capacity to innovate and to manifest.

Those whose soul purpose is to create substance may be interested in atoms and molecules—physics and chemistry. They may also tend to like to create substance as sculptors and jewellers do. In any case, Sphere tribe members love to manifest things tangibly, not just in theory. They may find themselves asking what holds substances together. A physicist would call it the strong nuclear force—a mysterious force that magicians must work with and master, if they are actually to create substance. Chemistry is a key function in this tribe as it works with atoms and molecules held together by the strong nuclear force.

Grid Tribe—tone of Bb—maintain connection

Grid tribe people tend to be highly intelligent and also intuitive. They may be dowsers or psychics, but more likely they are geometers, mathematicians, or crystallographers. They will find themselves interested in geometry, crystals, grids, and lattices. If you tend to find joy in angles, the Platonic forms, or crystals, your soul purpose may lie in maintaining connection. These people love mathematics and all the connections between numbers. They may also love pattern designs, as found in all cultures, or perhaps higher dimensional forms, such as hypernumbers. They may also tend to be an engineer or systems manager or educator in ways of using systems, sets or matrices. Maintenance of connection may also be keeping up communication with people, mailing lists, and filing systems.

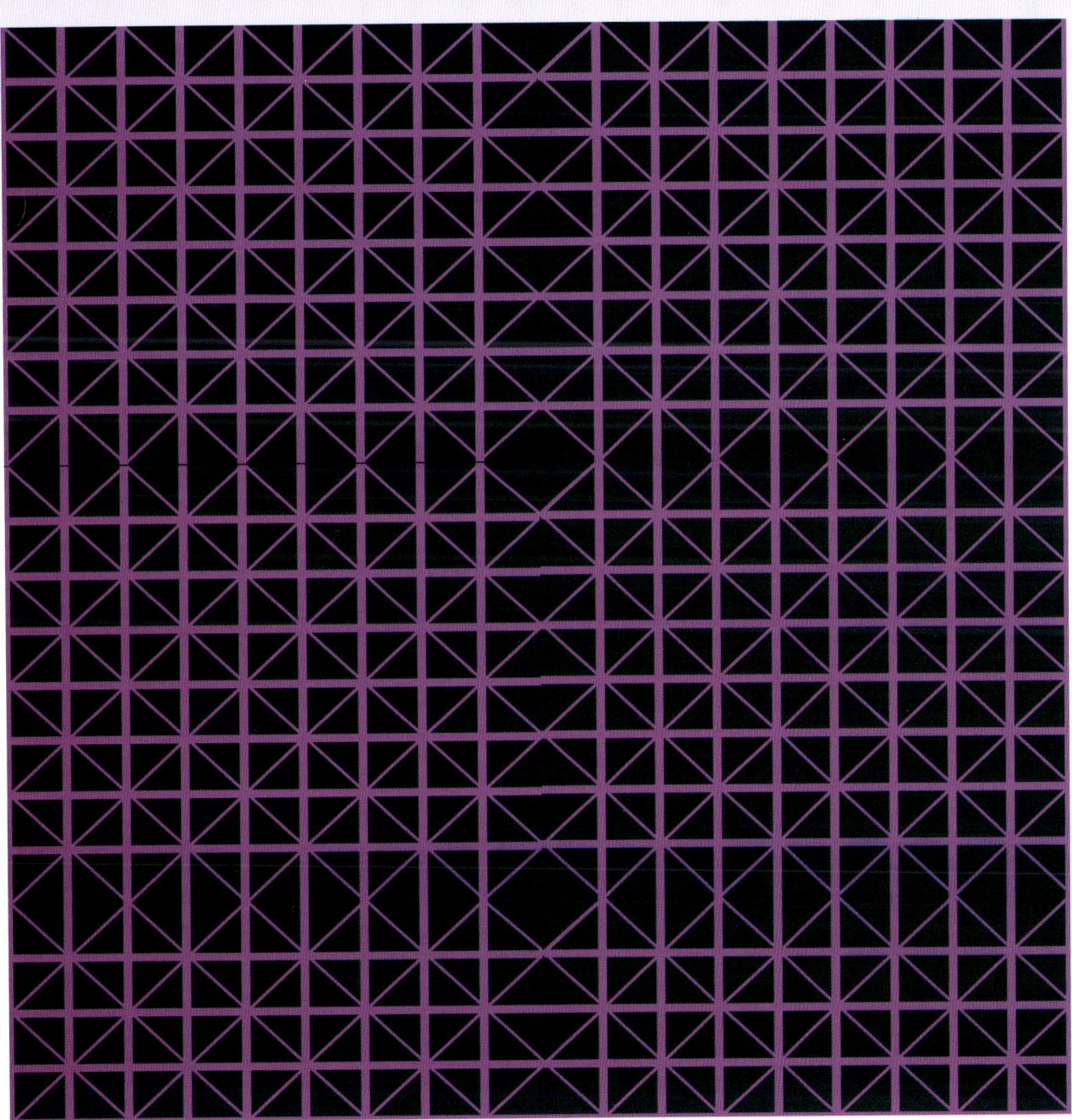

Mystery Tribe—tone of B—transform flow

Those whose soul purpose resonates to the Mystery tribe are likely to be rebels, poets, hippies or wanderers of some sort. If you feel this calling, you likely don't want to go with the status quo of society at all. You may be unpredictable and uncontrollable to family, teachers or even friends. The only professions you might wander into (and out of) are quantum physics or depth psychology or perhaps chaos theory, poetry, wild art or anything considered weird by society. This calling is not in order to shock or be weird, but just happens to appear that way to society at large. The level of reality related is the mysterious subatomic realm, which extends into higher dimensions, but does not appear to relate to ordinary three-dimensional reality. Such people are innovative in unpredictable ways, which may provide breakthroughs for those who follow.

Chapter Seven:
REN—FINDING A SPIRITUAL NAME
First Initiation

Finding a spiritual name, enables you to attune more deeply to your soul. There is a God-given spiritual name that you have through all lifetimes. By listening, praying and clear intent to find your spiritual name, you will be able to empower yourself to actualize more of who you are.

Sound comes from the primal vibrations of the universe in continuous creation. Sound is a current that runs through everything as energy flow. It is the primordial kundalini energy that rises through our chakras and it emerges through our heart, lungs, our larynx and mouth as speech. When we sing spontaneously we are most in tune with this primal sound current.

In an archetypal way, the different sounds that we shape with our larynx and mouth, are also represented by codes, energy flows, connections and substances. Our speech creates and combines various qualities through sound. The meanings or associations are secondary, for they have been acquired through habitual use. The primordial language attunes to the sounds themselves and how they arise. Listen to pure sound. Our characters have specific robes, based on their soul purpose. The robes they wear may help you to discover the sounds that resonate to your Ren.

GUTTURAL SOUNDS

Guttural sounds like H, G and K are the deepest sounds, coming from deep within the throat and lungs. They are inspirational sounds and ones that make a statement emerging from the inner life. These belong to the archetypes that represent codes and the fire element.

Ariel and Shawn represent two voices for the sound of H. The deep sound of H springs directly from the source of sound. The point too, originates deep within source. Its function is to create codes. Do you know people whose name has an H sound? Not the letter H as in Shawn, for an SH doesn't sound like H. Think of the H as a deep guttural sound as in the word hug.

Serafina and Francis archetypally stand for the G sound. The G is much harder than the H and is made by a kind of gulp at the back of the throat. Serafina and Francis's main archetype is the radial form that maintains codes. The word guttural has the G sound. Who are the people you know whose names have the hard G sound? G is a very strong emphasis of the sound current. It doesn't allow it through freely as the H does. G makes a statement. We are not using G as in George. That's a J sound. Words like Gregory, gasp, and give use the hard G sound.

The sound of K, whether spelled with C or K, is a hard krack! Humphrey and Clare represent this sudden K sound, which is visually represented by the diamond form. Who do you know whose name has in it a K? In many languages, the K sound is at either the beginning or ending of words. How do you feel about these guttural sounds?

Ariel   Shawn   Francis   Serafina   Clare   Humphrey

NASAL AND PALATAL SOUNDS

Nasal and palatal sounds like R, L, N, NG, and J are near to source like the gutturals, but they are shaped and emerging from the roof of the mouth and give qualities like water or energy flow. The sound current is shaped by the interaction of the tongue and the roof of the mouth. R is created by placing the tongue far back on the palate with a curled tongue. With L the tongue comes curled up against the palate. N and NG are sounded with the tongue more flat against the roof of the mouth, with NG being more nasal. J is almost a dental sound, but the tongue does not reach the teeth, so I include it here.

Ricardo and Jennifer represent the sounds of R and L. Their psychic attractors are the spiral. Ratta and David, whose psychic attractors are the wave, represent N and NG.

What words have these nasal and palatal sounds? The R and L sounds tend to roll or run like a river. Even the word lore has a certain current of tradition, flowing like a river. The N and NG are wavy like a current of energy flow. They tend to maintain what the L and R created. The sound of J as in Jones or John is represented by Ingalook and Radha as the transformation of energy flow, equivalent to the unpredictable psychic attractor.

| Jennifer | Ricardo | David | Ratta | Ingalook | Radha |

DENTAL SOUNDS

Dental sounds like D, T, TH, and S originate deep within the sound current, but they are shaped by the tongue against the teeth. They give qualities like air, for they are making connection with the outer world.

D is the hardest dental sound and it is equivalent to the column psychic attractor, represented by Dolores and Horus. Think of words like darn! difficult, dangerous, but then words like David, Dorothy, and Dick are quite neutral. How do you feel about interrupting the sound current with D? It's a strong statement, isn't it?

T and Th are represented by Wadabu and Joe, whose fundamental robe is the grid. T and Th are created with the tongue agaisnt the teeth on different ways. There are some languages that use many more sounds that I am ennumerating here, but this outline gives you a basis for finding your spiritual name.

S is almost a nasal and palatal sound, but it sounds with the tongue very near the teeth. Karen and Morgan represent S, which may be said to be the most soft dental sound, equivalent to the branch and the transformation of connections.

Dolores   Horus   Wabadu   Joe   Morgan   Karen

LABIAL SOUNDS

Labial sounds like W, B, V, and M are shaped by the air coming through the lips and the lips and teeth interacting in various ways. They are most like earth or the outer world manifestation of sound before leaving the person speaking. Labial sounds are usually soft, even though earth may be thought of as hard, but labial sounds are the most complete, fulfilled and manifest like earth or substance.

Shobak Shu and Janet, whose psychic attractor is the sphere, represent the W sound. The lips make the similitude of the sphere to make a W. W is made with an O shape of the lips. Winter, we, wait, wish, and names like Wilkinson and Walter are indicative.

Frank and Elizabeth represent the maintain substance function, with the psychic attractor of the step. B and V are the sounds made with the lips—in the one case bounding off each other and in the V sound, with the upper teeth touching the lower lips. These powerful sounds, as in the words, Bob, Victoria, battle and avalanche, truly manifest outwardly.

The labial sound of M is the most outward sound, coming from the lips pressing together and then releasing. Francesca and Ramon, whose psychic attractor and main archetypal robe is represented by the loop or torus, gives a sense of this completion and feedback. Words like Max, more, matter, mother, and matrix all begin with the M sound. M is often used as the completion of a word or mantra, as in AUM, HUM, and MOM.

Janet   Shobak Shu   Elizabeth   Frank   Ramon   Francesca

VOWELS

The vowels are really the sound-current itself as it coursing up through our chakras everyday and night—all the time. But different chakras shape them and we can shape them with our mouths as well as our intent and thoughts. They are the carriers of the sound current; whereas the consonants are the interruptions of the sound current. Find out what psychic attractors are involved in your name and then see the vowels as relating to the chakras as follows:

EIGHTH CHAKRA (and above)	silence
CROWN CHAKRA	AI as in I
THIRD EYE	EE as in eek or see
THROAT	E or A as in feather
HEART	A as in Awe
SOLAR PLEXUS	O as in Open
SEXUAL CHAKRA	OO as in MOON
BASE CHAKRA	U as is UP

Vowel Exercise

Stand upright and breathe deeply. Sound these vowel sounds from the base chakra upward and then from the eighth chakra downward. Concentrate on each chakra as you make each vowel sound.

Then glide you vowels together: U_OO_O_A_E_EE_AI etc and stay with whatever chakra and sound you feel you need for a longer time. Go slowly and find the diphthongs or intermediate vowel sounds and feel the sound current running through your entire energy bodies.

CEREMONY
Initiation for the REN

Each of our twenty-four characters seemingly represents one archetype. I say seemingly because people always combine numerous archetypes and some more dominant than others at different times of their lives. If, from your self reflection, you have a sense of which robe of light belongs to you (at least now), then play along with the dominance of that archetype at this time in the sequence of this book.

Each of the archetypal characters has a single "psychic attractor" robe. These robes are really their auric fields and show some semblance or quality of their inner life. As the soul resonates to specific codes, the energy emanates an auric field. In the ceremony they are to use their spiritual names, if they have received them. You might consider some of the qualities of the human voice sounds we have discussed on arriving at your own spiritual name. Or by simply asking the question, you may receive it spontaneously.

So now look at our characters in their simple robes. They are preparing for a ceremony as an acknowledgement that they even have light bodies! Each one says a dedication, in recognition of the quality of their auric fields. These are all just suggestions for you to create your own robe—at least in imagination—and to make a ceremony in which you make a dedication. Consider not only the beauty of the robe you choose, but also the consonant sounds that correspond.

Our twenty-four characters are gathered in a circle around a table with 12 elixirs. They do not know what elixirs are there, but they are attracted by resonance to one or another. Sophia is the overseer of this ceremony, for she knows what flower essences, gem elixirs or star essences are in the cups. Our participants cannot see or hear her, but likely they can sense her presence.

REN Exercise

Find out what chakras and what psychic attractors are in your common name and in your spiritual name if you have one. For example, my name ROWENA has the **Spiral**, the **Sphere** and the **Wave**. The vowels are in the solar plexus, the third eye (the E is pronounced ee), and the heart. PATTEE, my middle name, has the **Step** and the **Grid** as consonents. The vowels resonate to the throat (A is sounded a as in matter) and the third eye. KRYDER, my last name, begins the consonants with the **Diamond**, then the **Spiral**, the **Column**, and the **Spiral** again. The vowels for Kryder are AI (the crown) and U, the root.

After you work out which psychic attractors are in your name, you can draw or imagine a robe made of just those psychic attractors. Below is one version of the 66 combinations of two simple robes with the simple robes running the diagonal from upper left to lower right:

Chapter Eight:
THE KHAT, or HOLOGRAM of Your PHYSICAL BODY

Exercise: Scan Your Body

The first part of getting in touch with your Khat is to scan your physical body with your awareness. Either lie down or sit in a comfortable position and breathe deeply and slowly. First, just bring your awareness to the tip of your nose and be aware of the air as you inhale and exhale. This might be done for hours or days. Do it before going to sleep at night. The first part of this exercise will bring up Your Sekhem, the spiritual body that is an inherent aspect of your vital energy.

After feeling that you have accumulated subtle energy, begin scanning your body, inside and just on the surface, beginning from the crown of your head and moving slowly with your awareness into every part of your body. As you move down, go into your organs, skin and bones with your awareness. If you do this for days on end, night and day, you may begin to see with x-ray vision, your whole body and meet your Khat.

Chapter Nine:
The KA, YOUR SUBCONSCIOUS AND ETHERIC DOUBLE

Your subconscious receives and emanates subtle signals through sound and form, as well as feeling. Sound tones and intervals of sound penetrate the physical body, not only through the ears and brain, but through the entire body. You may have already attuned to certain patterns and colors. There are sound correspondences to these forms and colors. Nevertheless, your sound preferences or needs may be different from your visual preferences and needs. Just be honest with yourself in all the exercises and you will better be able to harmonize and integrate the light bodies you have activated.

The Ka is born with a person. As a double, the Ka is a harmonic pattern of a person. The human person can assume the form of a Ka after death, but it is not a soul. The Ka can exist apart from the physical human. Nevertheless, the Ka is the subconscious vital energy for the physical, and different Kas have different qualities such as strength, respect, glory, creativity, and magical power. Without this double, life is not possible.

We will explore harmonics and sacred geometry in this chapter. Using a Pythagorean tuning system, the following twelve-tone scale is derived.

Correlations of Pitch to String-length & Degrees of a Circle

Part of whole = amount of "string" sounding (plucked) Remainder = amount of string not sounding (not plucked)
This musical scale is the 5-limit prime "just tuned" chromatic scale with ratios comprised of multiples of primes 2, 3 & 5 only.

(+) means raised by syntonic comma at (81:80)
(-) means lowered by syntonic comma ratio of (81:80)

keynote	C	Db-	D	Eb	E	F	F#+	G	Ab	A	Bb	B	C
A:B = ratio	1:1	16:15	9:8	6:5	5:4	4:3	45:32	3:2	8:5	5:3	9:5	15:8	2:1
B:A = part of whole	1/1	15/16	8/9	5/6	4/5	3/4	32/45	2/3	5/8	3/5	5/9	8/15	1/2
Remainder = 1-B:A	0	1/16	1/9	1/6	1/5	1/4	13/45	1/3	3/8	2/5	4/9	7/15	1/2
part of whole X 360 degrees	360°	337.5°	320°	300°	288°	270°	256°	240°	225°	216°	200°	192°	180°
Difference degrees 360° - degrees	0	22.5°	40°	60°	72°	90°	104°	120°	135°	144°	160°	168°	180°
HERTZ (cps)	256	273.04	288	307.2	320	341.333	360	384	409.6	426.666	460.8	480	512

keynote	C	Db-	D	Eb	E	F	F#+	G	Ab	A	Bb	B	C
A:B = ratio	2:1	32:15	9:4	12:5	10:4	8:3	90:32	3:1	16:5	10:3	18:5	30:8	4:1
B:A = part of whole	1/2	15/32	4/9	5/12	4/10	3/8	32/90	1/3	5/16	3/10	5/18	8/30	1/4
Remainder = 1-B:A	1/2	17/32	5/9	7/12	3/5	5/8	58/90	2/3	11/16	7/10	13/18	22/30	3/4
part of whole X360 degrees	180°	168.75°	160°	150°	144°	135°	128°	120°	112.5°	108°	100°	96°	90°
Difference degrees 360° - degrees	180°	191.25°	200°	210°	216°	225°	232°	240°	247.5°	252°	260°	264°	270°
HERTZ (cps)	512	546.133	576	614.4	640	682.666	720	768	819.2	853.333	921.6	960	1024

by Rowena Pattee Kryder, October 2001; corrected by Randy Masters, January 2002

Exercise: The Sacred Geometry of Harmonics

Each of our archetypal characters has a characteristic tone, with its harmonic overtones (usually a trinity). Our experience of sound occurs both as speech and as music or tones. Speech may be thought of as various shapings and interruptions of one stream of sound. The stream is a current of harmonics that is cascading down throughout the universe. Various peoples have found diverse ways to play, rejoice and articulate the sound through their mouth and larynx. Examine the next pages, feeling what harmonics and forms you most resonate with.

You may or may not be a musician, but you can play the tones on a keyboard and then hum them. Go through the following twelve pages and discover which tones and sacred geometric forms resonate with you. Muscle testing is a good method to confirm or deny your own intuitive choices. To do so, make a scale of 1 to 10, with 5 being the norm. Some tones your Ka body may not need and others it wants. Muscle-testing is a Ka body method.

There are two ways to test your resonance with tones: based on intervals and based on specific tones. With specific tones, find a tone on a keyboard, then sing it and have someone muscle-test you. With intervals, sound a tone and then find its octave, perfect fifth, major third etc. and see what intervals your Ka Body is resonating to.

Then read the text of each geometric form and interval and allow your imagination to play in creating another dialogue on how you subconsciously resonate to each. The images given here are only a suggestion. Make your own images about how your Ka body feels.

The Harmonic Overtone Series

The harmonic overtone series is one universal method of attuning to the chakras and the Ka body. When you play a tone on a musical instrument, each tone has overtones that follow a specific geometric pattern. Let's say the tone is C, and number 1, then the overtone series just follows the sequence of numbers: 2 is the octave (C), 3 is the perfect fifth (G), 4 is the next octave (C), 5 is the major third (E), 6 is the next octave of the perfect fifth (G), and 7 is the minor seventh (Bb).

The overtone series is simply a subdivision of a string-length into smaller and smaller subdivisions. First 1/2, then 1/3, then 1/4th etc. This is just another way of counting 1 = C, 2 = C octave, and 3 = G.

In relation to the human body's Ka and the cosmos, it can be pictured like the figure to the right in relation to diverse chakras.

In terms of the chakras, the overtone series unfolds as C as ground of being, then C as base chakra, G as sexual chakra, E as heart chakra, Bb as brow chakra, D as throat chakra, F as stomach, A as foot chakras, B as crown chakra, Db as knee chakras, Eb as solar plexus chakra, F# as hand chakras and Ab as eighth chakra above the head.

A flat in relation to C is the closest harmonic interval to the golden mean (PHI) proportion.

(right)

A twelve-tone musical scale, relating to colors, and the functions of psychic attractors of each archetype, resonant with chakras.

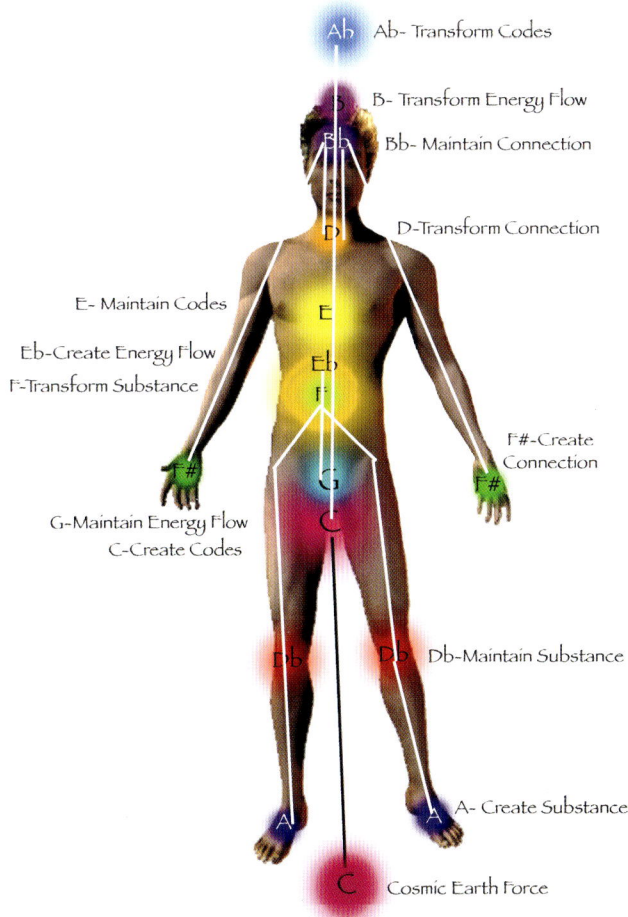

Ab- Transform Codes

B- Transform Energy Flow

Bb- Maintain Connection

D-Transform Connection

E- Maintain Codes

Eb-Create Energy Flow

F-Transform Substance

F#-Create Connection

G-Maintain Energy Flow
C-Create Codes

Db-Maintain Substance

A- Create Substance

Cosmic Earth Force

Octaves corresponds with Point and Zero°
C in Key of C

Though it is an exaggeration, in order to understand the intervals of harmonics, we can say that Ariel and Shawn sing only in octaves. To make it simple they sing only the tones of C in octaves. Of course they have different voices. Shawn's voice is not only deeper to begin with, but has more timbre or variations in harmonics within his voice. Ariel's voice is clear, higher than Shawn's and has fewer overtones. But they sing in harmonic octaves in a fiery light.

Ariel and Shawn sing of God's Love, for they know that is where harmonics originate, in the tone of C and the harmonic of one. All other harmonics originate from one. God is Love, which is creating with light codes. Photons appear and disappear simultaneously everywhere in a pulsating, scintillating universe. The octave: every point of light is a thought from God and to God. Within the sphere of creation, nothing follows a straight line. From a point of single vision within the center, a path is traced that moves in harmony with the fundamental of the tone of Prime Source/Creatrix, which emanates as Eternal Light.

The first archetype, inherent in all stars, is the single eye cleft in two and them reunited as eternal light that sees the codes or patterns in all things. The codes sometimes appear as Elohim, sometimes as the eternal light of the creative force; yet other times as creator gods and goddesses or as unicorns. By pointing the unicorn's horn in various directions, the angles of the radiation of stars changes according to the creative codes.

Your Ka, through octaves, is totally resonant with Prime Source.

Perfect Fifths Corresponds with the Wave and the Triangle
G in Key of C

This eternal light reflects inside the sphere of creation in trines, heard as perfect fifths. A fundamental principle is reciprocity: give and receive; receive and give. Reciprocity is expressed as a wave. The quality of the reciprocity is expressed as specific type of wave: square, triangular, or rounded.

Ratta and David sound the consonants of N and NG as rounds of perfect fifths, knowing that this interval is one of the most harmonious of all twelve. As they sound N and NG in alternation in fifths it begins to sound like waves.

A wave is a transmission of God's thoughts to and from point to point within a specific energy. This energy is all God's love and power from zeropoint, to measures of desire, to love of creation as it unfolds in waves. Every wave has a center that holds the zeropoint and is neutral. The wave transmits in a direction, but there is nothing moving: only the appearance of movement through the dual positive and negative electric charges, pulsing in the oscillating on and off of the universe. As Ratta and David sing their auric field radiates like the waves in their archetypal robes.

The sphere of creation circulates the waves of creation that are the voice of Prime Source as the *Logos*. Originally, the wave is the zeropoint, the immensity of the universe, and then it subdivides into octaves, fifths, thirds, and sevenths, creating the harmonics and grids that resonate with Prime Source.

The harmonics, angles and archetypes revealed in this story are continuously being created by the Logos, who is a trine harmonic with Prime Source. David asks Ratta, "What is the trinity of this interval?"

Ratta pauses and then replies, "The trinity is Prime Source, Creatrix and *Logos*, and it is the *Logos* who emanates the vibrations that archangel Raphael uses for healing, through the cycle of perfect fifths." She has studied music, and goes on, "Musicians call it the perfect fifth interval, but it is really a trine, for it is a subdivision of a fundamental string length into three."

This unending cycle made of trines, moves in a gradual displacement that creates a spiral of creation where spiritual water issues forth, keeping all-to-be-created in perfect nourishment and flow.

Your Ka, through perfect fifths, is in beautiful harmony with Prime Source.

Major Thirds Correspond with Radial and Pentagram
E in Key of C

The third fundamental principle is that God's love in every point radiates outward and inward. Every point radiates infinitely, revealing the oneness from every center everywhere. The radial is God's seeing everything at once; and every radial form in Nature can see as God sees: the oneness of all things. Serafina and Francis sing the consonant of G in major thirds, that is E in the key of C.

Francis reflects and mumbles aloud, "G is for God. The pentagram is a sacred symbol for God in life."

Serafina, overhearing him, says, "Yes, and the radial form that maintains codes, broadcasts the information of the point in all directions from its center. As a result of an infinity of points broadcasting, the rays intersect and there is an apparent expansion or explosion and then contraction or implosion. This is God's love radiating everywhere."

As Serafina suggests, the illusion of space and time is maintained by the circumferential force and extinguished by the radial force when the seer ceases to identify with any bounded universe. The radial is a simultaneous broadcast of God's love in all universes. The radial is the heart of God. Its center is still and its omnidirectional rays are also still. Implosions are simultaneous with explosions in the oscillating universe.

The paradox is that every universe is bound by a ring (circle) and yet is simultaneously one with every other universe. Space has no continuity, yet appears continuous from within each universe.

The Hyos Ha Koidesh use a sacred geometry, based on pentagrams known as the dodecahedron in the third dimensional world. The oscillating universe occurs from their ceaseless breath, loving and heart-beat of cosmic dodecahedrons pulsing into icosahedrons and vice versa. This is the heartbeat of the universe and the rhythm of the "metronome" that the god of light plays and sings to. It is this harmonic/geometric pulse that maintains the codes.

Your Ka, through Major Thirds, is in subtle harmony with Prime Source.

Minor Sevenths Correspond with the Grid and 160°
B♭ in Key of C

The fourth fundamental principle is that the expansion and contraction in the radial creates the appearance of space. Lattices of infinite reflection appear as grids or nets, the source of which is God's holy breath: inhaling and exhaling. In contraction appear neutron stars and so-called "black holes," which are really the space where space converts to time or rather, multiple times and dimensions.

Wabadu and Joe sing T and TH in minor sevenths, B flat in the key of C. Wabadu and Joe commune about the meaning of the grid, the sounds of T and TH and the minor seventh in music. Wabadu asks Joe, "A grid seems to me to be part of space, and space is expansion, isn't it, mainly?"

Joe, "In expansion appear the nebula and arms of galaxies out into empty space where God's exhale is fulfilled in ultimate expression of love. The T is like the phrase 'true to the T,' which also represents the Tao, the Truth and T has two right-angles in it, suggesting grids."

Below the wind force are the Thrones of God, for it is here that the angelic powers align in a divine geometry that maintains the connections through measures, ratios, harmonics and color. The nine muses, who are the weavers of creation, receive the energies of the Eight Forces from the Thrones and weave them into beautiful harmonic patterns. These patterns are carried by the crystal spirits into the atomic crystalline lattices of matter. They are based on the 3, 4, 5, 6, 8, and 9 patterns of atomic vertex and face angles. They use all the archetypal qualities created thus far: the codes, and the energies.

The lattices of crystals are manifest forms of the higher dimensional grids. In space, dimensions unfold from within outward. X-ray diffraction forms reveal patterns of higher harmonics.

Your Ka, through Minor Sevenths, brings in the first spatial dissonance with Prime Source, and yet longs for resolution.

Whole Tone Corresponds with branch and the Enneagram (40°)
D in Key of C

The Branch, the fifth principle, is that space and time are continuously branching out or choosing to move in, depending on the intensity and density of God's thoughts.

Karen and Morgan sing the S sound, hissing in whole tones, that is, D in the key of C. Karen reflects, "The branch is God's way of distributing love into the smallest recesses of the smallest entity."

Morgan, the inventor, is used to principles and laws, "The principle of recursive nesting is applied and the magnitudes of life, such as quarks within atoms within molecules within cells within organs within bodies within environments. The choice points of the branch can be seen at each node where the branching becomes smaller and smaller in incremental steps."

Karen resounds in delight, "Oh, I see! All growth proceeds from light received at each node of each branch. The veins of leaves have fine branches as a vehicle of the sap rising up to meet the incoming light."

The nine-pointed star emerges from the action of a 40° angle.

The Dominions are the angels who branch out, holding their ground, based on a love of God. Culture heros reach out from higher dimensions to distribute the wisdom based on principles and priorities. They move from the love of God to principles, to laws, to teachings, to tools. Culture heros use wisdom, shape-shifting, trickery, and love to awaken the stream of consciousness that leads to source, and that manifests the fruit of the tree of knowledge and life in culture.

To behold the tree of life is to go through the tree of knowledge, guided by a culture hero. This is to awaken qualities of discernment, prioritizing—extracting essence from the chaff of life. Behold what has been useful and cut through what is no longer of use. It is also nurturing the seed, allowing the plant to grow, and protecting the fruit. It is cultivation and distribution.

Your Ka, through the Whole Tone, takes a whole step toward Prime Source.

Perfect Fourth Corresponds with Loop/Torus and the Square
F in the Key of C

The fraction of the perfect fourth is 3/4 or a 270° angle. It is part of the 90° angle family.

Janet and Shobak Shu sound only the M, as a kind of hummmm in perfect fourths. That is F in the key of C.

Shobak Shu, wearing the Loop robe, ponders, "How is the perfect fourth in Western music related to the loop of feedback?"

Janet, "I know M is a mother letter. If the perfect fourth is 3/4, then a mother's love must be at least 3/4 of a child's life."

Shobak Shu, "And the Earth is our mother. Ecology or the interaction through a balanced food chain, is how our Mother Earth nourishes us."

Lake, as a spiritual power, moves down the dimensions to the angelic realm of the Erelim whose 90° angle births through angelic consciousness, the virgin and devouring mother. This is the womb where substance is transformed through cycles of apparent time.

Ecology is a feedback system of food chains where the devouring mother rules through the transformation of substance. This "digestive system" of the universe is essential for the metamorphosis and decomposition of substance, made of patterns of molecules. One realm feeds another, for the substance is not the essence. The essence is in the codes expressed in ever new forms through flows and connections, resulting in substance, which then cycles back to codes. Ecology, the feedback system of all of life, transforms substance by being the digestive system of a planet.

Your Ka, through perfect fourths, rebounds, and sounds like temple music.

Tritone Corresponds with Column and the 104° angle
F# in the Key of C

The column reveals the principle whereby every trajectory of every ray has a counter force, creating a column of sequentially repeated actions and reactions. The tritone is most dissonant with the fundamental and reaction is counter to action. The column is tension-compression, radiation-gravitation power. The pillar represents the spine of an upright human being as well as the tree of life.

Dolores and Horus sing the consonant of D in tritones during the ceremony. Dolores is a little uncertain of such harsh tones and consonants, "D is the hardest, densest sound in my mind and the tritone is extremely dissonant to the fundamental. The column is so uninteresting. What can we make of this?"

Horus replies, "Think of the central column as all-embracing Mind as well as the trunk of a tree. It must hold together many dissonant frequencies to stand upright. It is not biased this way or that."

Dolores is trying to understand, as Horus continues, "The stem or trunk of a plant holds the stillness of Mind within it. The elongation of a plant is finding a balance between light and gravity. The path of creating connection is standing still and witnessing existence while being in the midst of it, and it being amidst one's body."

Suddenly Dolores has an insight, "Oh! I see! The plants create the connection between light and gravity through photosynthesis and roots. Green, being the middle color of the visible spectrum, is the refracted color of photosynthesis in leaves. The plant realm is quiet, still and doesn't move except by growth. It balances extremes, and to befriend the plants is to find peace of mind, seeing clearly any given situation."

Creating connections is uniting higher dimensions and lower, light and dark, heaven and earth. The axis of the universe is in every creature. The column is in every cell as a spindle. It is a column of creative action where silent witnessing fears no extremes, and can thereby be resurrected by the pillar, which acts as a mediator between justice and the plant kingdom.

Mind, as a spiritual power, moves down the dimensions to the angelic realm of the Hashmalim whose 104° angle, births justice, Maat, the mother, who measures the soul against a feather, to behold its purity of conscience.

Your Ka, through the Tritine, feels extreme tension between itself and Prime Source.

Major Sixth Corresponds with the Sphere and Double Pentagram
A in the Key of C

Frank and Elizabeth sound the consonant of W in major sixths during the ceremony. The major sixth is A in the key of C and the sphere is the all-embracing, protective aspect of the mother. The gnomes are the elemental spirits that govern this archetype. It also relates to the nuclear force, the infinitesimal force that resists all matter returning to Prime Source, the One.

Elizabeth has something to share, "Couldn't we turn this statement around and say, the nuclear force is the love of Prime Source for the manifest realm of substance? It is eternal, consistent and powerful and can be used only by those who have immense respect for all substances. To manifest substance out of thin air so to speak, is to guide the gnomes concretizing spiritual Earth through the nuclear force. This is to love and respect matter, to know amethyst, tin, copper, and opal intimately from within the love of Prime Source. Isn't that so?"

Frank, "That's a profound thought. The extraction of gold, platinum, oil, and gems from the earth through mining may be spelling a death sentence to a planet. These substances are its bones and teeth, lymph and flesh. The gnomes know the treasury of different types of atoms and they create and protect the wealth of a planet through its substance."

The 144° grid made of ten-sided forms, is a higher octave of the 72° grid, made of pentagonal forms. The sphere and circle are among its forms, for the spiritual earth is magnetized to a center at close range. The gnomes gather and bond, creating substance out of spiritual earth by creating boundaries around every attraction to a center. Gnomes guard the atoms with their skins made of spiritual earth.

The spiritual earth manifests as the atomic realm. This archetype is intense and deeply bonded within itself. It acts at close range and has little awareness of the larger realms of space. The spiritual earth is a force that gathers substance to itself in small increments, silently and inconspicuously. Stillness is its quality and the Elim work ceaselessly and silently to accumulate and protect the gem-like qualities of the spiritual earth.

Your Ka, through major sixths, has a tension that reveals a harmony within its own center.

Major Seventh Corresponds with the Unpredictable and the 168° angle B in the Key of C

Ingalook and Radha sound the consonant of J in major sevenths. This is the tone that most longs to culminate in the octave, like the tone of B in the key of C. The form is what we sometimes call the laminar, but it is even more unpredictable than that, for it has no gliding of one film over another, but is true chaos and mystery.

To *transform flow* is the most flexible and unpredictable of all twelve functions. This archetypal quality is surrender to the mystery, the unfathomable, the abyss and void that transforms all energy. Transformation is a return to source, and through the teceptive force, the whole universe returns through zero point.

Radha is very thoughtful, "Is this archetype like the experiences of synchronicity and simultaneity?"

Ingalook continues questioning, "Might not uncertainty and chaos also be expressed as mystery, the unknown and the unknowable? Maybe with this archetype one reaches to the extremes of both hell and heavenly realms—dimensions below three and above three."

Radha, "I've heard that uncertainty is one of the principles of quantum physics. Isn't the subatomic realm below the threshold of knowing?"

Ingalook adds his wisdom, "In our old culture, all is created from the Void and returns to the Void. Ultimately, the subatomic realms must be rooted in the Void, called the vacuum by physicists. The Void is the ground of Prime Source and is also a plenum, a fullness, not an emptiness. Zero-point energy comes from this plenum, for all energy comes from the Void."

Radha, "Embodying this archetype is to access the flowing source of all energy and return it to that source and then to receive more. The Void is the alpha and omega, the beginning and end."

After a long pause, Ingalook rejoins, "One cannot cling to anything in this way, but must surrender to each moment in open trust."

The function of *transform flow* allows salmon to swim upstream in cascading currents and it brings about implosion where all opposites co-join. It is a fluid force of centripetal influence, for all inner tendencies open out into the subatomic where there is no foothold.

Your Ka, in major sevenths, is in its deepest longing for Prime Source.

Semitone Corresponds with the Step 22.5° (16-sided)
Db in the Key of C

The 22.5° is the smallest interval in the tones of the octave and makes for a sixteen-pointed star or geometric figure.

Francesca and Ramon sound the labial consonants of F, V or B with just a semitone above the fundamental of C. That is, D flat.

Ramon considers, "I think our archetype represents the gradual step by step approach to things. F, V and B are the manifesting consonants of substance. In a way this must also mean our archetype is more outward and material."

Francesca, "The states of matter—plasma, gas, liquid, and solid—must all be involved, don't you think? These could also said to be the constituents of solid, elemental planets."

Ramon, "Yes, I think of planets as the children of stars."

The Angelic order heading the archetypal function of *maintaining substance* is the Ophanim whose job is to create racheted "wheels" or "cogs" within cycles, that maintain substance in distinct dimensions, angles, and consequent types. Their consciousness streams forth to the builder gods and goddesses—those who create a step by step pattern of accumulation, allowing a build up of pattern-become-substance. Addition of layers by semi-tones is the way of this archetype.

The minotaur, on the imaginal level, is he who tests the walls of the layers. The layers of accumulated matter are circuits that appear as labyrinths. Waves of specific magnitude fit into each layer, which, when brought down to the physical level, become planets. Each planet has its layers of accumulated matter appearing as plasmas, gases, liquids, and solids.

Your Ka, through semitones, is extremely hesitant about harmony with Prime Source, but finds its way through a tension of dissonance.

Minor Third Corresponds with the Spiral and Hexagon (60°)
Eb in the Key of C

The law of expansion and contraction (or diffusion and compression) is that of generation and degeneration by the mediation of the spiral. The spiral is a trace of God's love mediating inner and outer. The minor third corresponds to a power of every center (point) to become what it innately is. In its becoming, it expands and diffuses its expression outwardly, while simultaneously contracting and compressing inwardly to be what it is in essence.

Ricardo and Jennifer contribute the L and R sounds in minor thirds to the ceremony. Jennifer says, "I always feel a sadness when I hear the minor third chord. It is poignant and deep, stirring emotional unfulfillment."

"But the sounds of L and R are among the most lively and stimulating of the entire alphabet," joins in Ricardo. "I feel very attuned to the spiral and its generating ability."

Jennifer, "Yes, L and R sounds really move."

"They even spin or roll," answers Ricardo.

"Maybe the sad or poignant quality of the minor third is the pivot point around which the energy rotates to create flow." Jennifer is reflecting more within herself than answering Ricardo.

The function of *create flow* works through a hexagonal 60° grid governed by the B'nai Elohim, the children of the creator angels. The Elohim and the children of the Elohim create flow as a spinning of energy. To spin is to generate energy. Whether through an electron around a nucleus of an atom, through planets spinning around a star, or as stars whirling around the core of a galaxy, this archetype generates the flow of energy.

What is energy but a circulating of codes in ever widening or contracting arcs? Expansion is weakened. One begins to feel lack not having enough support, nurturance, and love. The energy flow of the B'nai Elohim is rooted in love. The codes cannot penetrate into the core of galaxies without love. The nagas are magnetic dipoles bringing love from the vortices of the nurturing goddess who creates galaxies. The spiral galaxies are the symbol of the archetype of *creating energy flow*. For spirals generate new stars in the three dimensional universe, which is the display for the global computer.

Your Ka, through minor thirds, feels sorrow about itself in the universe, but moves ahead in poignant peace.

Minor Sixths Corresponds with the Diamond and the 135° Angle
Ab in the Key of C

Humphrey and Clare sound the strong K in minor sixths, in the ceremony.

"I feel good about this archetypal quality, for it is the last one in the harmonic overtone series. It also relates to the 5:8 proportion—the ratio closest to the golden mean of any of the twelve intervals," says Clare.

Humphrey, "Yes, but I'm puzzled by its relation to the 135° angle, which is part of the square family."

Clare, "It is really something that the K as a guttural sound, relates to codes. Maybe we don't understand what is really guttural, gutsy, or deep."

Humphrey, "There must be a more rational answer to my question."

Clare seems to be thinking aloud, "The minor sixths correlate to the human being. The human is manifest last in evolution, but it is said that the human was created in the image of the divine. What does that mean rationally?"

Humphrey, " You may be on to something. The human is said to be conceived perhaps through an energy like the guttural sound of K, but becomes manifest through the 'square' angles and then transforms his/her own codes to return to Source."

Clare, "That's a big thought. I think that is the hero/heroine's Journey."

The Hero's Journey reveals the archetypal path of recognizing social injustice, undergoing a deep underworld journey, meeting one's shadow, then emerging to confront the evil-doer, and bringing a boon to the social order. The boon is of wisdom in action—inwardly and also in the world.

The Seraphim are the angelic order of this most highly transformative archetype. It is the centaur in the imaginal realm that is the symbol of integrating the human and animal realm while aiming for pure spirit. It also relates to the spiritual soul of the human that has the potential to regenerate and redeem all the human corruption of the ages.

Your Ka, through the minor sixth interval, concentrates its power within itself and resonates to Prime Source from within.

Chapter Ten:
THE KHAIBIT
Fourth Initiation: Your Unconscious Shadows

In this initiation, you need to be willing to look at your own unconscious patterns. What are you defending? Are you making judgements about someone or something? Judgements have emotional charges with them. Discernments are able to evaluate without an emotional charge of desire, fear, or hatred. Examine what you are defending. Do you hate someone or something? Are you angry? What is the root of your anger: hatred, expectations, frustrations?

The Khaibit forms its own judgements based on past experience, but if the conscience is not clear, the Khaibit's evaluations may be illusory, and therefore dangerous to your whole being.

Look at each character's extreme emotional face in the following twelve pages. Which ones do you most identify with? Which ones repel you? Which ones remind you of something, someone, or an experience you have had? Read the inner life dreams of each character's unconscious and feel if any of them resonate with you, or have in the past.

Integrating the Khaibit is one of the most profound and significant initiations. Of course it is not usually done all at once. In the following pages you will glean a few indications of your character's shadows. A synopsis and a piece of a dream or nightmare is given. Make note of your own dreams, both conscious and subconscious. Attempt to understand what your desires and fears are.

How do shadows come into us? Either in the present incarnation or another one, there is/was a hurt from a frustrated desire, or a wounding by another, or by circumstances. The hurt becomes anger, the anger becomes hatred and resentment, and eventually the whole emotional charge goes underground, into the unconscious. The Khaibit as shadow is often denial of hurt. To recognize and accept hurt is to bring the denial out of the shadows into the light of consciousness and feeling again. It is better to be in some pain than to feel numb, to lose sensitivity and awareness. Being alive and aware means feeling, but not always identifying with the feeling, or taking it personally.

Each of our characters responds to life in a different ways, so their Khaibit weaves a different myth, a different story, a different way of coping with the pain of life. If you can uncover the quality of your Khaibit, and hear its story, you are a long way toward integrating it. But you may not always believe its stories.

KHAIBIT EXERCISE

1) Ask two friends to play two roles in your unconscious: one an ally and the other a shadow. These should be friends you know and trust, and who know you. The one who plays an ally is to affirm all the qualities you need to empower you to be fully who you are in essence. The one who plays your shadow is to detect qualities that may be unconscious to you. Open yourself up to these friends and reveal what upsets you, worries you, makes you react, feel a victim, or makes you arrogant. Bring forth all the truth you can about your "dark" side. Recall times of your childhood when you were cruel to others, hit trees, hurt animals or anything else that you may regret doing, but can acknowledge now. What is hurting you now? What frustrations do you have?

Now the three of you put on masks (paper bags might be colored) and play out the unconscious drama. Your shadow is to bring up all kinds of trying things, and your ally is to bring up supportive qualities you can draw upon. Let this drama unfold as it will. Now, standing between these two, how do you feel? What comes up for you? How can you reconcile these differences?

2) Pray at night or early in the morning, for insight about your shadows, about qualities you previously denied, but now can acknowledge and transform. Ask for dreams that help you release obscurations to being who you really are. Feel and witness. Feel and witness. Detach, but feel, and your shadows will dissolve and your Khaibit will be informed and integrated.

Ariel is unconsciously angry. Old hurts and insults about her ability to excel transform into anger when she feels helpless to change. At times she feels absolute rage and fury about the discrepancy of her visions and her ability to manifest them on earth. This she knows. What she does not know is that her anger is rooted in a fear of existence itself. Unconsciously, she is not sure she deserves to exist.

Falling from a great height, her dread emerges on the way down. She sees twisted bodies of horses and humans all entwined together within the shapes of the cliff side. As she feels being crushed, she awakes.

He is crawling in a tunnel, a sewer, in order to escape. Wholly alert, he crawls on and on. They are after him and will burn him if they find him. No time for thought, just alertness and pain. Seeing a light ahead, he crawls towards it. When he emerges, they take hold of him.

Shawn cries and laughs at the same time. To calm himself, he writes. His consciousness penetrates into the deepest recesses of each person, animal and thing. Unconsciously, he finds existence itself to be painful, for his sensitivity is so extreme that he loses his balance between perception and expression. He is so perceptive, he cannot express to other people what he sees and feels.

Frank's inner life implodes in parallel with what he does on the outer. He is aghast at the complexity of existence and unconscious of his soul's purpose. He works patiently and hard everyday, but is beginning to wonder what the point of it all is. He suffers from self doubt and covers it with activity.

He dreams of being ploughed under the earth and waiting for centuries, like a stone. People pass by, not noticing. He feels amazed when he awakes, for he seems locked in a space where no time passes.

The children are playing in the street as she drives home. Suddenly, one leaps in front of her car, chasing a ball. She awakes with a horrible fright that she has run her over.

Elizabeth has been everywhere she wants to go, done everything she wants to do, but is wondering if she missed something. She is secure, insured and has all details taken care of, but is unconscious of how well-loved she is. She loves nature and children and a few people.

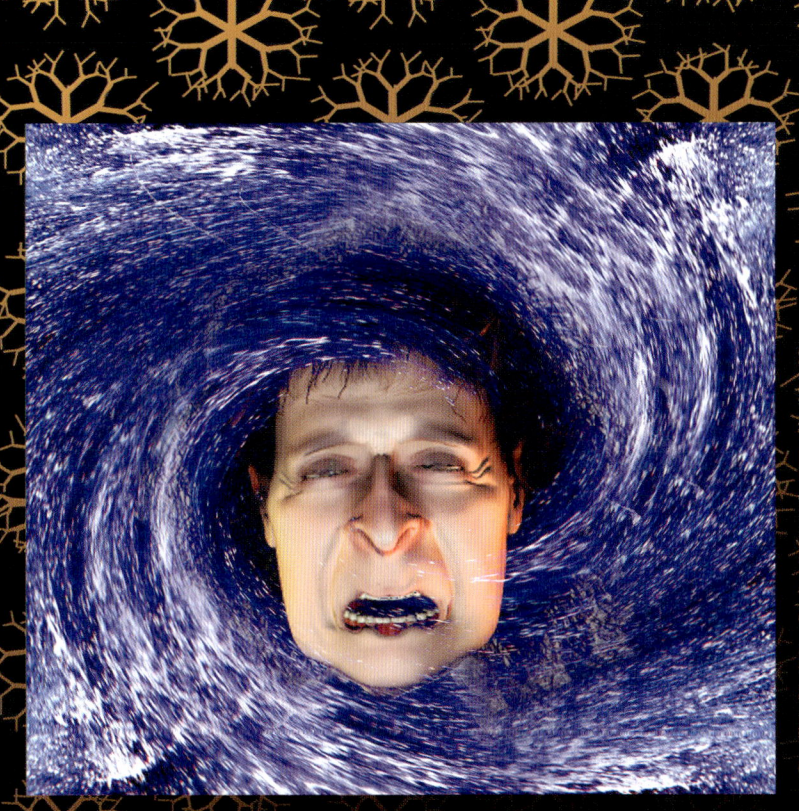

Karen worries whether she can accomplish everything she wants to do. At times she feels overwhelmed, anxious and breaks out crying. She feels in a turmoil . She forgets herself in the process.

Leaving herself out of the equation, she overextends herself, gets rundown and often is ill. Feeling at once driven and stressed to the breaking point, she falls into a depression.

She dreams she is caught in a tornado over and over. Sometimes it is being swept down a drainpipe or a whirlpool in the ocean. Something huge is about to swallow her. As she awakes she feels helpless.

He drifts in space, without orientation and fears falling. Falling to where? There is nothing but the void, vastness, infinity. He drifts on and on with a terrible anxiety. When he awakes he feels dizzy and disoriented.

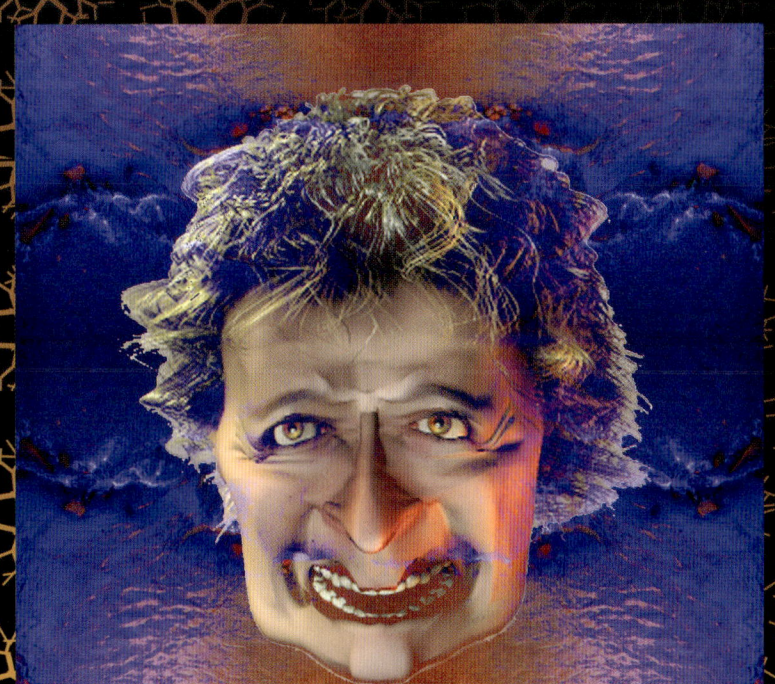

Morgan is so ambitious that he agonizes over the limited means he finds at his disposal. He wants order and form, which require limits, but his own limitations bring acute anxiety. He blames the outer world for not supporting his endeavors.

Unless he is creating order incessantly, he fears he will be carried into oblivion.

Ricardo is afraid he has become so sensitive to other people's needs that he doesn't fully know himself. In his most worried moments he rides horses. There are many people around him who admire him and who depend on him for direction. He is unconscious that he has made them dependent on him, so that he can feel useful.

There are crowds of people shouting. He is a gladiator in Rome, fighting for his life against both armed men and wild animals.

She dreams of being locked inside her own house. She tries all the doors and even the windows, but they are all sealed.

Jennifer has become rather smug and indifferent except when she is dancing. She lost her husband and her son when they went on a skiing trip in the spring and were killed by an avalanche. The pain inside devours her, for she is unaware that this very pain is what can bring her to life.

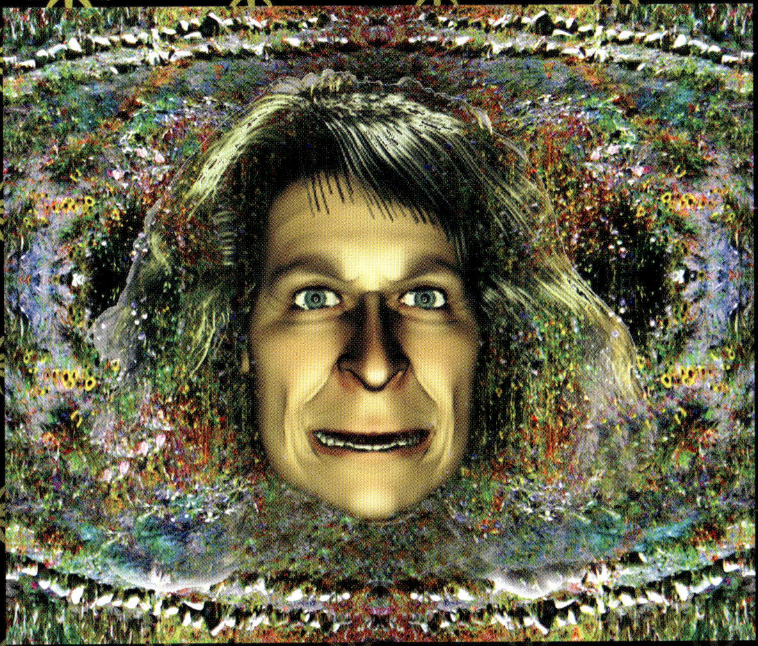

Serafina is having an intense time, for she fears that her former radiance is dwindling. She is painting dark abstracts, unconsciously attempting to draw her out of coming face to face with her doubts about herself. Her actual spirit is more penetrating than ever, but she is used to trusting her physical beauty, and has difficulty accepting her spiritual beauty.

She dreams of a lion devouring an antelope, and then going to sleep in a dark cavern. In the afternoon the lion vomits, and at night, the antelope comes back to life.

He dreams of being tied to a fiery pyre with cannibals dancing around him. Suddenly he surrenders and he hears a sweet voice singing.

Francis is explosive even though he is highly disciplined, for the depth of his unconscious is erupting like a volcano. Frustrated and ashamed, he attempts to control his feelings, but he cannot. Unknown to his conscious mind, his release of ancient traumas is enabling a rainbow ring to radiate around him.

Franchesca is extremely worried, mainly about her children. though she strives to be detached, she is not. She finds solace in gardening and water, for she feels as if she is experiencing internal combustion. She is critical of other people and cannot help being judgemental.

She dreams of being lost in a cave, unable to find light. As she wanders in the dark, she beholds a fire deep inside the cave and she wants only to put it out.

He is inside a chamber where there are electric switches everywhere, going off inside and outside of him. He cannot turn them off, so he keeps switching them on and off.

Ramon is so sensitive, he sometimes plays macho to compensate for his feeling and intuitive capacities. He is wrestling with new ideas all the time, for he cannot find peace within himself. He finds momentary pleasure in competitive sports and in overcoming others.

Dolores has consternation over injustices in the world: starving children, the greed of large corporations, the lack of education and opportunity for all. She has an unswerving stare, and yet she hesitates about every decision in her life. She is unconscious that her indecision is rooted in fear of failure.

She cannot make up her mind about which door to take. Both are glass, so she can see inside. In the left door there are crying open mouths; in the right door there are beautiful gardens. She awakes in confusion.

He is lifting up a building and has to balance it or the people inside will not survive. He carries it across an abyss to a cliff bank, and his back is aching as he awakes.

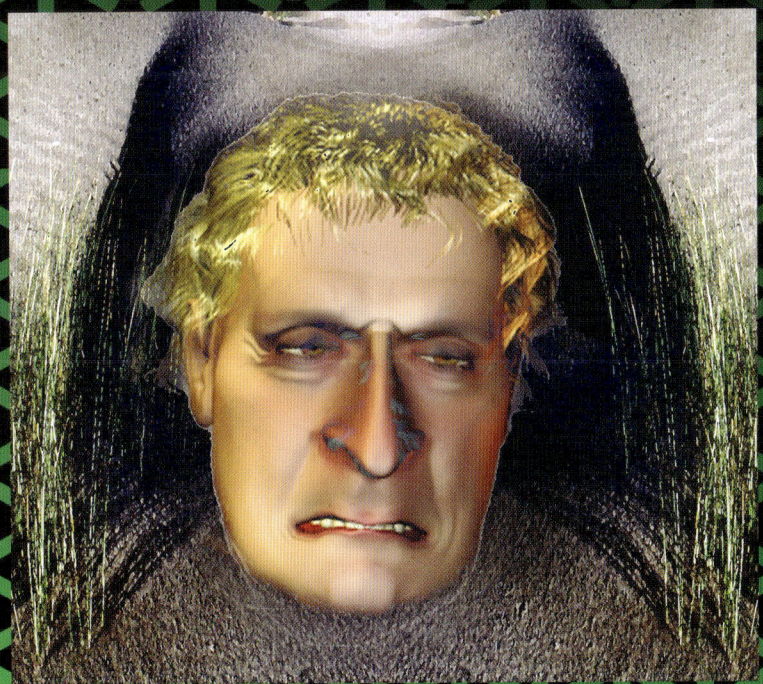

Horus helps refugees as a lawyer, but he wants to do something more in direct contact with the people he seeks to help. As he takes a trip to India, he is deeply affected by the general poverty in many cities and rural areas, but even more, he is amazed at how happy the people generally are. He enters a dark cave to contemplate what happiness really is.

Ratta has consternation about her personal life. Two marriages have gone adrift and she has no intimacy with anyone, though she acts as a counsellor to many. Her desires are still intense, but are bottled up and she feels pain in her body. Sometimes she feels as if she were burning up.

She dreams of ecstatic skies and feelings and then plunges into volcanic dust. Wandering in the dust, she finds a hole and enters, sitting in the darkness. She awakes, alone and afraid.

Caverns and caves are filled with squirming snakes and worms. He sees children ahead and involves them in a game they make up together. He hits one of the children with the ball, by accident.

David is a coach to college basketball players, but is frustrated because he wants to create beauty. Taking up painting and also guitar playing, he creates chords and patterns that swirl in wild abandon. His teachers try to impose discipline, but he chooses to learn by himself.

Humphrey is very internalized, even though he is approachable by people of all walks of life. Unconsciously he has an existential terror. He fears that the universe is infinite as well as eternal. This is terrifying because the infinitesimal is essentially identical to the infinite, so there is no sense in achievement at all.

He dreams of sliding into a waterfall and, seeing the bubbles, he enters inside and beholds atoms and the atoms disappear into a dynamic flux of subatomic particles and he awakes in terror in a vast Void.

She walks through crowds, hearing everyone's thoughts. They are like firecrackers going off everywhere. Ahead, just ahead is a cool pool, but she cannot reach it.

Clare's heart is open so she sometimes picks up dark thoughts of others. In her effort to delve into the essence of each soul, she has anguish about the human condition. She studies myths to find some redeeming quality, but is afraid she will never find it.

Shobak Shu is sorrowful, for he has lost all his known relatives. Unconsciously, he makes up for it by finding threads of wisdom and power through various indigenous peoples. He is an old priest and suffers from there being no real priesthood for him now. His sorrow is an attachment to the old ways.

He dreams that he lost his drum, and is powerless to heal the animals. He wanders for a long time and sees a geometric pattern that opens his higher mind.

She dreams of building a wall with bricks. The bricks are heavy, and the mortar she uses doesn't hold them together. When the wall falls, it crumbles and buries people. She feels fear as she awakes.

Janet was judged severely when she was young. Unconsciously she knows she is limited in every way and that she needs to organize her life to make herself worthy. She has headaches and feels guilt for some unknown reason. She works very hard to help others.

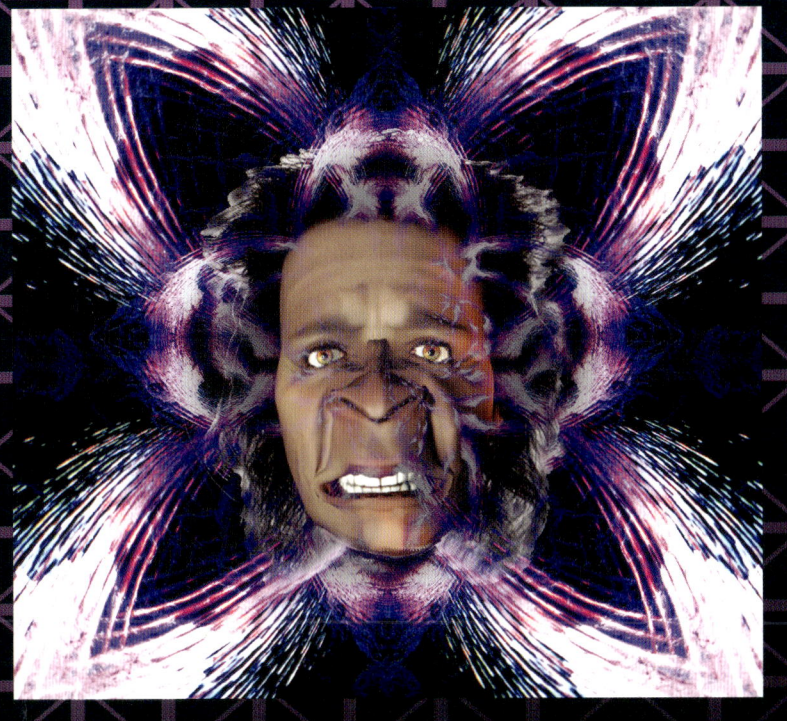

Joe feels like the center of a cosmic experiment. The myths of his ancestral people help if he could believe them, but he turns to technology to solve his and the world's problems. He is unconscious that technology is only an extension of his own consciousness.

A machine is pulling him into a central hub. He has the key to turn off the machine, but he is fascinated with the effects it might have. His movement is slow, unending. He is unable to turn the key.

Over and over the same dream happens: she is caught in a grid that has no up or down, right or left, forward or back. How can she find where she is?

Wabadu sometimes feels helpless about racial problems when so many have such hatred of people who are different from them. The genocide in many places in the world, frightens her. Unconsciously, she hates herself, for she has an ancestral mix of diverse races, which others have judged.

Ingalook has a deep sorrow, that is not even so unconscious. The reality of his body, his subconscious and his unconscious are all in deep feeling about plants and animals. The pain of not being able to do enough for them gives him an ever-present ache in his heart.

He dreams of being lost at sea, but it is a sea of animal parts—legs, brains, organs—all swirling in a chaotic sea. He cries in the dream and his tears merge with the liquidity of the body parts in the sea.

She twists and turns in bed as the smoke fills her lungs and her cells scream out in searing pain. Her dream brings her into a tangible sweat and deep inward charge that takes her hours to dispel.

Radha, having been burned at the stake many times in so-called past lives, is now suffering from fiery memories. Unconsciously, she loves only the Void, for it gives her a sense of peace; whereas all other beings or states of being, bring her to a fear of attachment and loss. Her mother was incapable of love, and only her soul has given her the courage to live on.

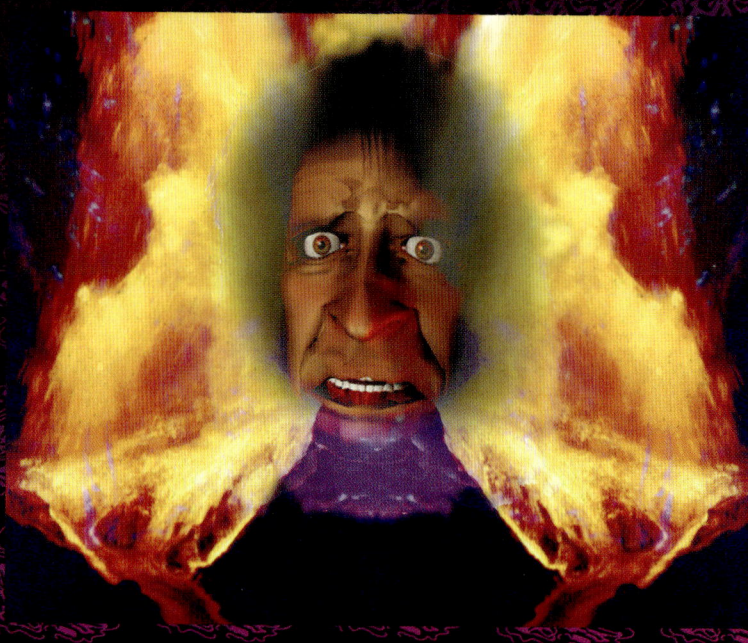

Chapter Eleven:
STORIES OF CONSCIENCE

Fifth Initiation: The AB, Your Conscience

With the fifth Initiation, we find our characters seeking to clear their conscience. They are still wrestling with their Khaibit, but are on the way to taking responsibility for their thoughts, and feelings, not only their words and deeds.

Forgiveness is a key to turning the Ab and letting it reflect the soul in the heart. Examine yourself and reflect on any conflicts you've had with others, with the law, or with the way your life is going. What is at the root of any such conflict? Look at small things: irritations with people, impatience, speaking impulsively in a way that hurt someone. Why have you done such things? What is at the root of any such behavior, speech or thought?

AB EXERCISE: How Is Your Conscience?

The Ab, as the conscience, requires absolute honesty with yourself, and a willingness to release all secrets, judgements, fears and desires. This does not mean you have completely released all, but that you intend to do so, truly are willing to do so.

There are various settings for this exercise, but camping and building a fire at dusk is a good one. Create the fire in such a way that one log rests upon another (which is somewhat inevitable with a campfire!). Say a prayer, speaking to your Ab deep within yourself. Something like: "I am intending here to clear all grievances, all wounds from the past. Here me now! This fire is my witness. The stars and trees are my witness. The earth, this ground of sand and rocks is my witness. I intend to acknowledge and clear past traumas this very night. Keep me honest, even if some part of me doesn't want to be."

Light the fire with this intention or other honest intention you have, and at first watch it flare up. Observe the logs and wood as parts of yourself that you can release and let go of now. Let past grievances burn up and return to the light as fire. Ask the fire to tell you when you need to remember a hurt you'd done to another, or something another had done to you. *The fire does this whenever one log burns through enough to let another log fall. When it falls, you will remember*. The log falling is a sign from the spirit world that you have insight now and can forgive. This is self-hypnosis. This is fire remembrance.

Walk slowly around the fire praying for forgiveness. Keep walking. If you need to sit, then sit. Put another log on the fire after each one falls. Time after time, remember any time you ever hurt anyone or anyone has ever hurt you. Feel in your heart how it feels to be the other person, how they felt when they hurt you or when you hurt them. Let the fire burn up all the hurts, all the consequent anger and hatred, revulsion, confusion and pain. Let it all go. Stay up all night if there is more to forgive. Do this ceremony repeatedly if you do not yet feel clear communion with your Ab.

Ariel

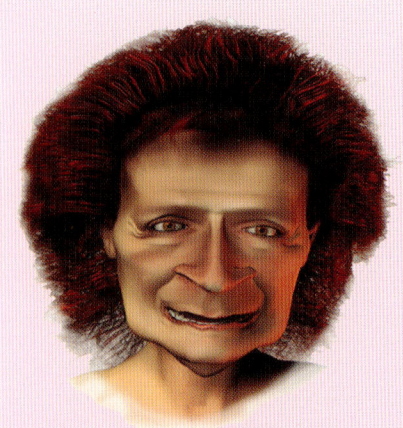

is going through intense trials. For one thing, her vision is vibrating in scintillating colors. It may be migraines that happen when she is under stress. Although she reaches for divine light, her will is so strong that she has difficulty surrendering to Divine Will.

"What is Divine Will?" she asks, "If not through my will? Passivity cannot be the way!" She has made friends with Dolores.

Dolores' Ab says, "Perhaps divine will comes when you are not willing or even looking."

"What do you mean?" replies Ariel. "We know so little that goes on within us. Perhaps your will is unknown even to you? I know what I want!" exclaims Ariel.

Ariel spends sleepless nights wrestling with her Khaibit (shadow). She fears the voidness of existence and lives through the nights in dread. Her energy is so strong, coming to peace happens only after long hours of tossing and turning. But when she ceases trying, her surrender is very deep.

She prays, "Forgive me for being so willful, stubborn. There is still something that I dread. But I don't know what. Forgive me any transgressions, known or unknown."

She has had kundalini experience since her twenties and she has very high inspiration. Painting and visual graphics have become a godsend for her as an outlet for her passion. But she is frustrated at her art compared to her inspiration. Art helps to ground in that it is a manifestation, but it is still coming from her head.

One sleepless night her Ab, her conscience in her heart says, "What do you want?"

Ariel replies, "To be a divine eye, to be an eye for Prime Source, to bring forth beauty from the fountain of truth."

At that moment, Ariel is totally honest with herself and opens to the truth. Her Ab comes nearer and whispers, "Then dedicate yourself to that."

Shawn

suffers from over-sensitivity. He is learning the harp, singing and discovering more about his feminine nature. Shawn is learning to soften his intensity and spends long hours out in Nature.

Shawn speaks to himself, "I believe I can make music from tuning into these plants. Ferns have a rhythm in ascending and descending tones. The pine trees are like radiant sounds of horns. Look at these violets. They sing softly like soft whispery harps."

Shawn's Ab smiles. It is becoming evening. Birds are singing and a hawk swoops close by. His Ab says, "that is a sign of recognition. Your inspiration is now strong."

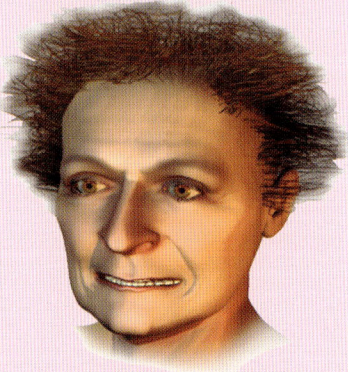

"Yes, but I have difficulty in expressing my insights among people who do not realize the beauty of Nature. I find myself reverting to my strong, male role, and even make my voice deeper and more growling than it really is."

Ariel's Ab, "The more you love Nature and see its patterns of creation, the more you will naturally express its inner nature. You are becoming androgynous."

Shawn reflects on what it means to be androgynous, and is unsure whether he can acknowledge a gay tendency he has, publicly.

Shawn's heart becomes a receptacle of the seeds of life. The flowers, the earth, the sky are all receptacles. The sky darkens and the moon rises. He prays, "God, please forgive me for hurting all the people I've hurt, but most especially forgive me for eating animals without gratitude, eating plants without appreciation. Help me balance my masculine and feminine sides. Give me the grace of clear direction."

Elizabeth

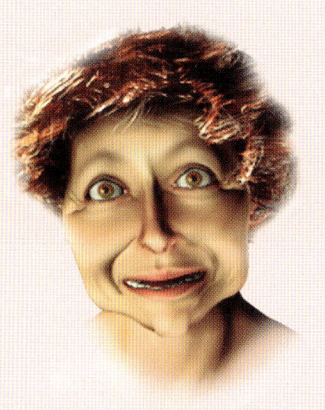

has three children who have left home and she is lonely. She wants to care for something or someone. Her husband was killed in an auto accident. She has had much grief in her life.

"Why do I feel grief and sorrow? I have had a good life. But what now? I have lots of life yet to live! What to do?"

Her Ab is felt deeply in her heart. It wells up from the depths in the early morning: "You are loved, but you don't trust it."

That very day she volunteers to help at the school in the library. After a couple of weeks, two of the teachers call to say they want to meet with her. When they arrive at Elizabeth's home, they are courteous, but one begins to say, "We appreciate your help, but you seem to get attached to some of the children and impose ideas about books. And they want to be left alone. We've had several complaints."

Elizabeth looks aghast. "I didn't know. I just want to help."

The other of the two teachers assures her, "You are helpful in filing away the books, entering data in the computer and showing children where books are if they ask."

Elizabeth breaks down, "I'm always doing the wrong thing. Forgive me. Perhaps I'll do something other than volunteering. You needn't worry."

That night Elizabeth prays, "Please dear God, give me insight on how I can be of use and yet be detached enough to not bother anyone."

The Ab within her heart says, "Don't give up. You are loved more than you know. Continue with the library work and look around you. Many children love you."

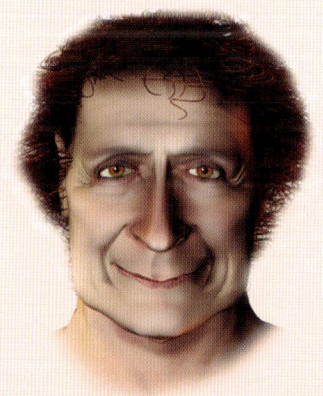

Frank

The search for fulfillment in Frank's life goes on and on with many outer results, but few inner satisfactions. His conscious mind is out of touch with his Ab. His head does not know his heart.

Frank has made lots of money and with all fairness to his customers. He has not deliberately hurt anyone. He feels his strength, his abilities, and yet he doubts himself.

The people around him are used to seeing him work, work, work, but one day he doesn't work. A neighbor comes by to see what has happened. "Are you ill, Frank? What's the matter? Why aren't you working?"

Frank's reply is, "I've decided to take week ends off. I haven't done that for twenty years. I think I will go fishing."

At the stream where he goes to fish, Frank is quiet all day long, talks to no one, and sees no one. The sky, the trees, birds, and water all penetrate into his heart. He camps overnight, and on the second day, he begins to feel a deep peace he hasn't known in his entire life. He is in awe of the beauty of Nature and realizes he has wasted much of his life being driven with activity.

That night, in his tent, he prays inwardly to himself, to his Ab, "Forgive me for being so insensitive, so closed, so mute, so driven." He sees that he has been working himself to death because of his father's expectations of him when he was a teenager.

When he returns home, his neighbor, who has become a friend, looks at him in astonishment, "You have changed, Frank. You look so much younger, and happier."

Frank smiles to himself. Now he communicates with his Ab every morning and evening, and whenever he awakes at night. His Ab is a stream of happiness at being included in Frank's life.

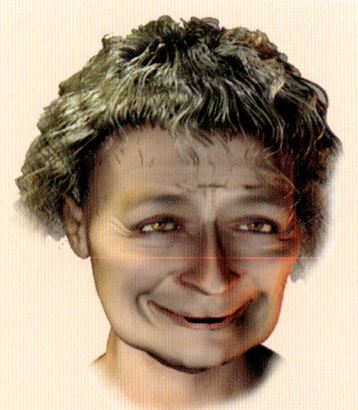

Morgan

feels his Ab in his heart and the discrepancy between his Ab and his life causes him great anxiety. He has many choices to make: about business, new inventions, patents, but all of these are fading in his consciousness. There is still a dread and anxiety gnawing at him.

He finds a new woman partner, seeking to ease his anxieties through her, but it leads only to more expectations, frustrations, and anger. So now, on a trip abroad on the plane, he turns within himself, "Why do I find no peace in this work? Why has my personal life suffered so much?"

He opens his heart to himself, "I know about engineering, structure, geometry, patents, business, but I still don't know about my soul. Is there a soul?" He doubts. "Every woman I have a relationship with leaves after and year or two. Why?"

As he dozes off in the plane, his Ab wells up in his heart, "You are sensitive, but won't admit it. You are loving, but don't know it."

"What can I do?" he awakes with a start, "Who are you? How can I know you?"

His Ab replies, "Appreciate the structures that you invent as part of God's creation as you did when you were young. Love people for who they are, not for how they are of use to you."

Suddenly Morgan sees, "I am always seeking a reward, not the thing itself. Forgive me this confusion. I see now. I will change. Even my inventions are not my own." Morgan begins to find release and relief in this insight.

Karen

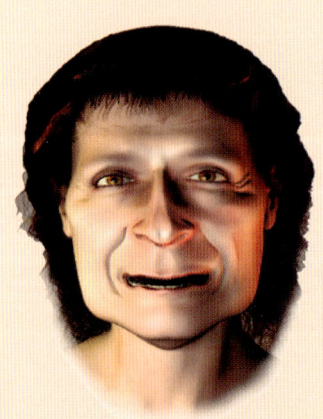

still has fits of being overwhelmed and feels she needs to build up her strength. She is working on exercise, diet and life style changes. She no longer goes to parties to ease her sense of loneliness, but feels as if her life is harsh. "I can do so many things, and yet I feel lost. I work like crazy and yet life gives very little back to me, even though I have enough to live comfortably. I just don't understand why I still feel overwhelmed at times, and frustrated at others."

One time when she had a cold and decided to stay in bed, she cried, "Oh, I wish I could feel better." She dozed off in a fever.

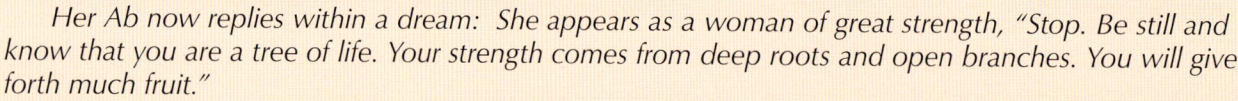

Her Ab now replies within a dream: She appears as a woman of great strength, "Stop. Be still and know that you are a tree of life. Your strength comes from deep roots and open branches. You will give forth much fruit."

When Karen awakes, she feels her dream is natural and a deep part of her. For a while, she holds the dream in consciousness and drifts off again. Her Ab begins to open in a way she never felt before. She begins to feel a new togetherness within herself. She doesn't feel the familiar need to be extremely busy. She sighs. "What if I just quit?"

She feels a strength emerging through her sickness. Her Ab speaks directly to her consciousness, "You are a tree of life and can fulfill everything just by being and responding naturally to situations as they arise. Rest awhile."

Gratitude wells up in her heart. She felt this way only once before, when she met the man she married. But since then, even her marriage has gone by the wayside in her frenzy to accomplish. In gratitude, she murmurs to herself, "I begin to feel how being a tree of life accomplishes everything in accordance with my heart."

Jennifer

has lost a sense of joy since her husband and son died, but she wants to come back to life. She is giving dancing lessons to children, but doesn't have the same verve as she once did. She despairs that she may never feel that ecstasy and life she once had.

In the midst of modelling the dance steps for her young people, she becomes frustrated and thinks to herself. "This is not life! This is not ecstasy! Why take them through the steps, if they don't enjoy it?"

As the children are about to leave, she asks them, "Is this dancing fun for you? Tell me truthfully."

One child frowns and the others all nod. "What do you feel, Alice?" Jennifer asks the frowning one.

"I like dancing in our meadow better. I need more freedom." answers Alice.

"How about our practising three days a week here and two days a week in the meadow, or forest?" All the children smile.

That night, as she is preparing for sleep, Jennifer is more sorrowful than ever. "Why didn't I see that the young dancers were losing their sense of joy?" She feels acute pain from closing down from the pain of her personal loss.

She drifts off to sleep as her Ab speaks through her heart. She dreams of dancing in the forest, among the blossoming fruit trees. She feels such love for her husband and son that she knows that love is eternal. Her Ab opens her heart once again and the children are happier also.

Ricardo

has lost all sense of direction in his life. Being an abandoned child, he has sought to be everything and everyone to people he helps. He has made his clients dependent on him and consequently they become angry when he is not there for them. He is still considered a valued member of his counselling team, and he now teaches clinical psychology at a college. Yet, he knows his own inner child is as needy as ever.

Confused, he retreats and goes on a trip to South America where his ancestors are. But he doesn't know them. He is seeking roots for himself, for his soul and heart.

He wanders through Peru. He doesn't even know where his ancestors are from. It doesn't seem to matter. He is here, in a "foreign" country and yet feels more at home than in the United States, where he has lived all his life. He walks the high peaks of Peru, through brush and trees, with groups and by himself. He doesn't want to talk to anyone, even though he learned Spanish in high school. The natives don't speak Spanish and he feels an acute sense of emptiness and loneliness, a sense of being abandoned, by his parents, by God and by everyone.

He just watches and witnesses his own agony and pain of being abandoned. He allows himself to feel it intensely. As he approaches a little stone temple, built ages ago, he is so moved that he calls inwardly to his own heart, "With this gift, I am blessed. I release all sense of abandonment, for happiness is here."

His Ab speaks, "Whether here or anywhere, you are a child of the Great Source. No longer do you need to have others depend on you, for all have source within them."

Ricardo begins to see how happiness is from within and that God has not abandoned him. This releases him from needing others to need him.

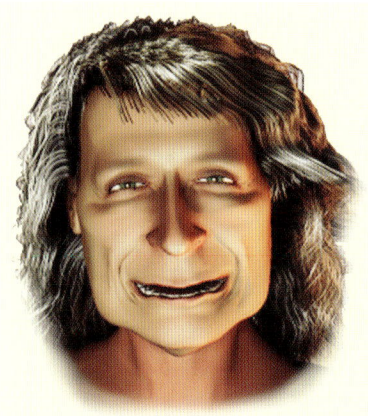

Serafina

is having a mid-life crisis since her aging is showing. She hasn't really trusted her beauty, her inner beauty. She begins going to parties and dances to meet more adoring men, but it doesn't work. She comes home weeping and sorrowful, not knowing what to do with herself.

She awakes five times during the night and weeps every time. She calls out from the depths of her heart, "How can I find peace and beauty, joy and happiness again?"

She drifts off to sleep again and sees many shapes and colors that appease her for a time. She dreams and forgets dreaming.

During the summer, she decides to go on a watercolor expedition to national parks by herself. She goes to Glacier, Yellowstone, and Yosemite—all places of great beauty, dear to her heart. Watercolor is a difficult medium because it is not easy to cover up so-called "mistakes." In her younger years, she painted in diverse mediums and styles, but was never fully satisfied with any of them being an expression of her soul.

As she camps out, the fresh air, skies, trees and rivers begin clearing her aura of sorrow and self-doubt. Under the open skies, at night, her Ab speaks within her heart, "Your beauty is within. Reveal the beauty to feel and see in color and form."

She paints everyday for two weeks. At first the paintings are stiff and washed out. Gradually, as she accepts herself more, her paintings are fluid, subtle, and brilliant. In this way, she purifies herself of self-doubt and begins a new hobby and career for herself. Her soul reveals her real beauty through color and form.

Francis

has a fair balance of yin and yang, inner and outer most of his life, but now that the Earth is moving closer to zero-point, he realizes deep anger is erupting. The inner is coming out. His poetry is becoming wild, explosive, with rhythms and rhymes of disparate words. His poetry no longer "makes sense," but it makes music and speaks to his Ab:

"What, where, who is the needly sparks that have no home, barking, sharpening, shaking and shuddering to the bone?"

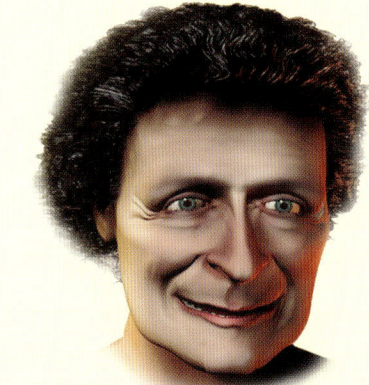

His Ab replies, "In the center. Find the stillpoint, the no-will point where radiance shines without making, baking, doing, or stewing."

Francis is amazed at his own senseless language coming back to him and enlightening him about his oscillations. He suddenly sees that all pain in his life is from a resistance to being one with the One. The fiery volcanic emotional reactions begin to cease and he wonders how such intense pain can be changed so suddenly.

Having studied physics, he realizes that even matter, the atomic nuclear force within his own body, resists being one with the One, while being within the One. "How can, how can anyone with a physical body, feel one with the One?"

His Ab replies, "Your heart-consciousness knows its oneness with the One."

He makes a prayer at night:

"Dear One within all! I ask for help in the release of all resistance to becoming one with thee, to being one with truth, one with love, one with beauty. Help me let go of all interference to thy Oneness."

As he continues this prayer, night after night, his poetry becomes clear and beautiful, even if nonsensical, for it speaks to the heart more than the rational mind.

Francesca

has suffered from judgements of others and from judgements of herself. She knows judgement is usually a projection onto others from oneself, but she can't stop doing it. Deep down, she hates herself, and it is this that makes her feel she is in a fiery furnace or is self-combusting.

Having undergone scientific training in botany has made her more critical, skeptical and fine-tuned, but when combined with self-hatred, these qualities become judgement, instead of discernment.

Francesca cannot see how to overcome her resistance to balance and wholeness because she is so highly conditioned that the truth cannot be from her heart. The truth to her is always from the brain. The only thing in life she opens up to is plants. When she was younger, she could see and feel nature spirits, but that has long since been conditioned out of her by her scientific training.

It is to the desert that she goes for solace. Southern Arizona is where she empties of all her hatred. She finds herself speaking to cactus, "Tell me what is the root of my unhappiness? I see that you just are who you are, and even if you are cut, you don't seem to suffer. Or do you?"

She ponders a while, as she moves through plants with spindly branches, tall ones with bristles, others with long sharp pointed leaves. Her Ab speaks to Francesca, "None of us are apart from Source. Source supports all of us. Do you feel and know Source?"

Francesca prays in her own way, "Let me feel no separation from Source, and make no judgement." Gradually she becomes more at peace with herself.

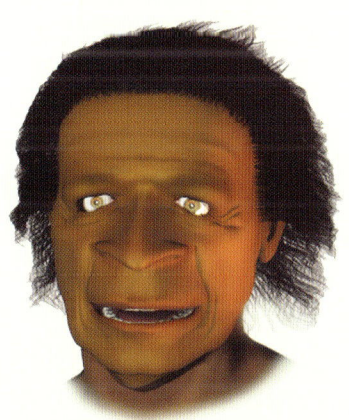

Ramon

is still filmmaking, but he is becoming more and more reactive to situations and actors that don't move the way he wants. He gets angry and emotionally fights every situation that does not go the way he planned it. He used to be spontaneous, but as he has gotten older, he has more and more expectations.

Because he is so intense and feeling his Latino cause, he has difficulty accepting that his movies are not chosen for awards. He also has nervous disabilities, for being yang and creative all the time is exhausting. Now he seeks rest, peace, and receptivity. He takes time off between films and wanders the streets, observing people, just being receptive.

His Ab speaks to him when he sits on a street corner, "Your genius is a gift, and to use it is to be open to change, other viewpoints, and seeing the unity flow through."

It comes to him as a thought, but unsure what this means, he just walks the street block and watches. He sees business people, high school kids on skate boards, old ladies shopping. "There are many stories right here," he says to himself. He makes notes of what he observes and makes up stories about people he sees. Sometimes he asks the people about their lives to see how similar his story is to their truth. For a change, his next major film is a documentary about a woman who takes care of disadvantaged children. He gets very involved just accepting the truth of the situation and letting go of expectations.

Many months after this experience, he gathers his actors and crew for another dramatic feature. He apologizes to his crew for being too demanding, stubborn, or forceful. Everyone sees that Ramon is making a change toward greater receptivity and openness.

Now, Ramon has a new method of directing: He grounds each actor in their character, creating ever new situations for them to respond to making up their own lines. He trusts each actor to be the character they represent, and be creative in the moment, just as he is. The film unfolds with much less effort than before.

Dolores

wants justice for all, but of course that is not happening in the world, so she tries to help people who have been victims. She has been serving as a mediator for eighteen years, and has reached a certain level of fulfillment in doing that. But she still feels frustrated that the world seems so unchanged for the better.

She begins to realize that she can't change the world, and that she can only change herself. Dolores searches her own conscience for imbalances, injustices she has inficted on others.

Dolores is finding that in her childhood she felt herself a victim. Her older sister and brother always put her down, made fun of her, treated her as inferior. She was also raped once in her teens, and vowed to help other rape victims. She has done so, but still feels unfulfilled.

She goes on a trip to Europe with her daughter. Finding distance from her work, she becomes more objective and also more able to listen, being receptive to her own inner voice. One night, as they are staying in a Bed and Breakfast in northern Italy, she hears her Ab speak, "Find the fulcrum from which you balance extremes. The root of your fear is in failure to help, yes, but more, fear of being a victim."

Dolores wakes startled. She doesn't think of herself as a victim. How is she a victim?

Again, her Ab speaks in her sleep, "Victim consciousness is not satisfied. Some want revenge, others want to help and cure. All you can do is be."

Horus

keeps his composure no matter what happens. There have been many times when injustice prevailed, when he lost his law cases, when opponents attacked him when he did win. He has grown tired of antagonism and seeks to find the middle ground.

His trip to India opened him to a certain simple happiness that he had never known before. Amidst the poverty and lack of amenities or even cleanliness, his ancestors on his father's side showed him the simple delights of stories, songs, colorful garments, gardens, unusual food, and laughter.

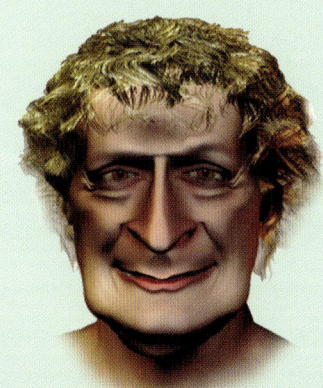

Horus wants to introduce more of these simple pleasures into his own life, but is not sure if he deserves them. Oddly enough, he is overly zealous in his law work because he is uncertain of himself. He wonders, in silent moments, whether he is really worthy of simple happiness.

His Ab is coming closer and closer to emergence. One night he hears a thought within his heart: "You are essentially happy. Actualizing it in existence is just a matter of acceptance."

"Acceptance of what?" is his question.

"Accept yourself as you are."

"How am I?"

"Your greatest gifts are just being who you are. Your secondary gifts are naturally helping others."

"Am I to cease being a lawyer? Can I continue law while being true to myself?"

"You have done so already. It doesn't matter whether you continue law or retire to India, or any other place in the world. Just be happy."

Night after night, day after day, Horus prays for truth and happiness and because he is honest and listens to his Ab, he receives more and more truth and happiness.

Ratta

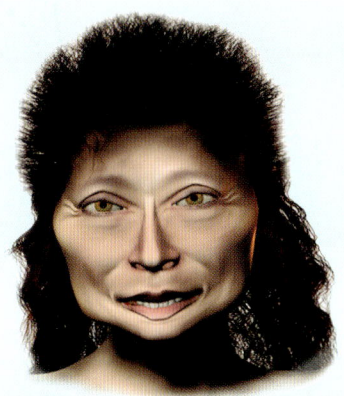

has become a successful psychiatrist, but is frustrated with her own personal life. She knows the root of her issues, but cannot seem to change. Yet she trusts none to help her, though she assumes people will trust her when they come to her. This paradoxical situation is at a stasis and deadlock when Ratta decides to go on a fling in Hawaii. She takes three weeks from her work and goes alone, and anonymously, dressing in flamboyant dresses, shirts and slacks and wandering through the forests and hills of Maui. She begins to feel as she did when she was in her twenties. She is open to anything.

One afternoon she comes upon a hut in the jungle and is intrigued with the blue-eyed man resting inside behind mosquito netting. He smiles and she smiles back. "Do you live here?" she asks.
"Yes, for now I do. I'm enjoying the simple life on my way back to the States from India."
"What do you do here?"
"I go for walks and meditate. Would you like to go for a walk with me?"
He is barefoot and the jungle is full of prickly plants. Ratta takes off her shoes and socks. They walk and sometimes nearly run through the forest. With every step she releases distrust, though her feet react in pain. She feels this wild adventure is a gift. They are both silent. It takes complete attention just to live, knowing where to put their feet in each instant. She feels her inner child is present and happy.
When they return, she tells her story, her frustration, her distrust of men. Yet her Ab speaks through her, "I feel completely at ease in your presence, running through the wild with you and being here now."
He smiles and they make intense love on the hard bed in his hut, saying nothing.

David

is very gifted in many ways, but in the middle part of his life, he wants to create beauty more than involve himself more in sports. To get involved with art or music means having enough financial reserves to be able to learn for a year or two. He is in conflict about being supported enough to do what in his heart he really wants to do.
Every night he thinks about this problem. One night, his Ab speaks to him, "If you follow your intrinsic joy, you will live in happiness. Be frugal. Cut down on expenses and also have trust that you will be supported."
His Ab, being another aspect of himself, is very clear, but his fear of lack, keeps him in conflict.

He talks about this to the administrator at the college where he coaches. The administrator speaks matter of factly, "Make a choice yourself. You have served well these past twenty years. You will not receive benefits if you quit now, but perhaps we can hire you in the summer months."
David, "Really? I would welcome that."
On his way home, he is clear that he wants to compose music, sing and play guitar. David opens his heart to be able to trust that all will be well if he follows his joy.
When he arrives home and tells his wife about his decision, she is adamantly against it. "Singing will not pay the bills!" She doesn't want to live more frugally than they already do.
David struggles with his unconscious fears that night, "I am aware of your force, but I have a heart and soul to be fulfilled while I still have interest and vitality. I will not give in."
The next morning he speaks to his wife, "My dear, I will give you more than half of what I have made, but I feel it is right for me to be free of obligations. We have some savings for retirement. You can have it. Whether we separate or stay together, I will create music and sing."
His wife cries, but does not leave him.

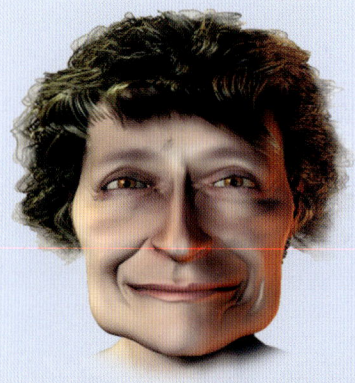

Clare

has been a university instructor and professor for many years, and now wants to write a compendium volume about the universal themes in world mythology. She loves her students, at least most of them, and she is very inspiring to the young, but Clare takes on levels of their consciousness, even they do not know. She embraces each student with compassion and also understands their souls.

The academic world has not been responsive to her search for universal themes, for specialists want others to be specialists.

Clare has gone on sabbatical in the academic world and is writing from her own voice. But she misses the students. One day, three students come to her house. "Please come back to teach us. We don't have anyone but you who really understands us. So many of our classes are just routine, linear and don't make us think."

Clare smiles and invites the three students in. "I've been thinking about the theme of death and rebirth, that life is impossible without it. All the cultures have this theme and it is always tied in with a culture's theory of creation. I am taking a sabbatical now, so I may or may not come back to teach at the university. This may be a death to you, but it is a rebirth to me. When I return I will have many more riches to share with you. Meanwhile, you can come on Sunday afternoons and we will discuss your ideas." The students smile and walk back to the university.

The passion and love in Clare's heart is stronger than ever as she writes at night. Her Ab speaks to her as she writes in a trance, "Unless people go beyond their minds and risk the danger of madness, there is no death and rebirth and no re-creation of a culture. Dynamic peace is ecstatically alive."

Humphrey

has inherited wealth, but wishes sometimes he had a regular post at a magazine or newspaper, so that his writing spreads into the world a little more meaningfully. His second regret is that he is unhappily married. He doesn't want to hurt his wife by divorcing her, but she knows he doesn't love her.

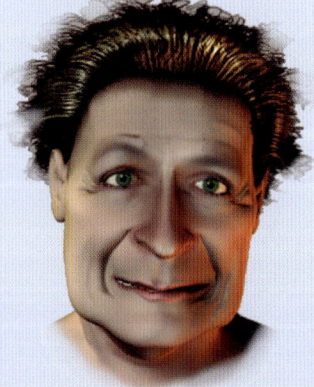

Humphrey is not really attached to much of anything, but he has everything at his disposal, everything outwardly that is: house, ranch, horses, wife, money. But he is unhappy.

One night, the estrangement between him and his wife is particularly acute and he decides to sleep in the spare bedroom.

During the night, he feels as if he were slipping into the Void, that nothing matters, that to do anything is ridiculous. He prays, "Dear God, Void, Truth, Whoever you are. Help me see the value of my life! Give me orientation! Give me insight on what turn my life is to take now! Help me care enough to do the right thing! Help me release all interference to being true to myself and fair to others!"

He feels as if he were spinning, spinning in space when the Ab in his heart replies, "Be sincere and you will know what to do."

In the morning, Humphrey feels more clear, that his life has more meaning. Then he realizes he has already decided to get contact publishers and submit his writing. He will get a city apartment if necessary.

He speaks to his wife, "I am going to hire another hand to maintain the ranch. I need to publish my writing. All these years, only five pieces have been published. I want my work to be in circulation. I am too detached from the world."

His wife replies rather bitterly, "You are detached from me too. What do you plan to do about us?"

"Our relationship will go wherever it will. I only know that my heart says to write and to publish."

Janet

feels more and more fear as she gets older, and yet she is more and more helpful to people and animal causes also. She begins to realize that all her life she has depended on other people's opinion of her as a guide. And since there are many people with different opinions, she is becoming ill with this approach.

She goes on a long hike every evening and during weekends and finds clarity is just being outdoors in Nature. It is on these long walks that her Ab opens up in her heart and speaks to her, "Allow yourself to feel any disturbance or conflict. Detach from the results of your work. You are not what you do for others."

She is amazed that such thoughts come to her, but it feels right.

Janet feels disgusted about all the different views people have about how the institute might be organized or run, where to get volunteers, who to probe for money, and so forth. She has managed such things for years and allowed everyone to have input. Now she feels that acting as assistant CEO for the Institute means taking charge and listening, but not always being swayed. Her Ab arises in her heart whenever she gets more clear, "Your love of animals and Nature is your most clear guide. Listen to your associates' views, but then find the wisdom in yourself to proceed."

She realizes, with regret, that whenever she has let someone take over because she wanted to please, it has been disastrous for the Institute's purpose, which is to spread knowledge of, and implement the rights of animals. She prays on one of her walks, "Forgive me for wanting acceptance from others. It does not work, and is not true."

She cries and walks and walks and cries until all the need for acceptance is cleared. Then she realizes that if she accepts herself, and trusts the process of feeling clear, all is beginning to be well.

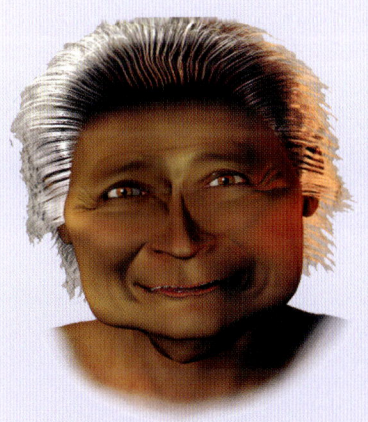

Shobak Shu

still has sorrow over the decline of traditional peoples, but he is beginning to find his power. There is a conflict in the village between two brothers, one of which seeks the new ways of technology and power and the other of which clings to the old ways. Shobak Shu, now an elder, is asked to sit in council to mediate this conflict. He is apprehensive, for he has never been in such a decision-making position before. That night, he speaks to his Ab through his heart, which he knows well. "Show me the truth, no matter what I prefer."

His Ab replies,"You have yet to stand in your power. These brothers have other wounds from each other and from others, that keeps then reactive. Make ceremony for their healing."

The next day the council sits together with the brothers present, to find a solution to the problem. Five elders speak for one side or the other. "Let the brothers separate. One will go into the white man's world and let the other stay here." But the brothers have a hidden love for each other that Shobak Shu sees.

When it comes time for Shobak Shu to speak, he says, "Let us make ceremony and invite the spirit guides of both brothers. Let us drop our own views and see what happens when we make an offering and invite the guides to preside over the ceremony. If you like, I will drum."

The whole village comes to the ceremony. First there is an offering. Then the guides are invoked. After that, the brothers each have time to speak, show, declare, or make any statement they wish:. One brother says, "I'm fed up with meaningless traditional ways. I submit to this ceremony only because of our mother. I don't want to go off to the white man's world. I don't fit in there either. I want my brother to come with me and together, we will find a new way."

The other brother says, "I am afraid of the white man's world and I see no need to leave here."

Shobak Shu asks them to lie down and journey with his drumbeat to see what their guides say. After the drumming, both brothers have tears in their eyes, and they embrace.

Wabadu

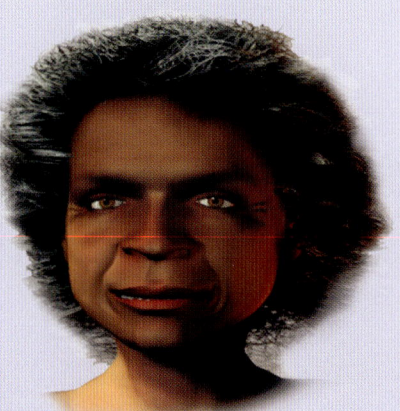

is happy when she is working with mixed races and they begin to harmonize, but often they don't. She still feels every judgement people have for people different from themselves, especially racial difference, but she understands it is from self-hatred.

Wabadu has travelled all over the world except Asia. She seeks to promote racial and cultural understanding. She studied psychology a few years back, but did not really find what she sought.

When she goes to Africa, she lives with the black people and hears their stories. The HIV issue there is so extreme that Wabadu feels almost in despair, but works on helping with sexual education.

While communing amidst a tribal ceremony, her Ab speaks to her, "All hatred is self-hatred. All judgement is some aspect of self-judgement."

"How can I enable the people I meet to know that?"

"Choose to be completely free of self-hatred yourself."

Wabadu realizes now that when she feels judgement of others, there is some aspect of self-judgement within her. She then feels unaccepted and unaccepting. This takes her into a space of disorientation and confusion.

She prays, "Great One Above All, I surrender all judgement, all hatred right now! If it ever comes up, I pray that you take it away. I release it from my psyche here and now. Help me to be loving and compassionate everywhere I go. Give me the strength and courage, to be clear and true."

Joe

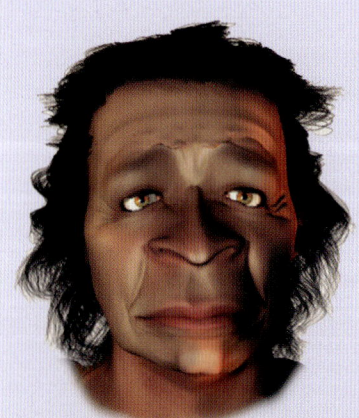

is struggling with the possibility of stepping down from technological research and simply having a teaching position in a small college. It would mean half of his salary, but he is happiest when in interaction with people. He has been doing neurological research, finding how memory works and how the brain develops.

Now that he is in his middle years, he is finding that such research does not tell him what he really wants to know: How is it that certain memories stand out and others are obliterated? The relationship of brain to mind is still a mystery to him, after many years of research.

Joe is married and supports a family, so changing positions has strong consequences for his family, but his wife is understanding, "If you are happier working with students, then do that. We'll manage. We always have."

The key that he could not use to turn off the machine in one of his dreams is found in dialogue with his Ab: "I feel bad, making my family suffer from my choice to teach college instead of getting big research grants and salary for brain research. I understand more about how the brain works, but still am in the dark about how the mind works. What can I do?"

His Ab replies, "The root of a tree is invisible, though without it, the tree would not grow."

"You mean mind is like the invisible root and the brain is like the tree?"

"The source of mind is God in your heart. The brain is a means, a mechanism. Cease mistaking the means for ends. The end of mind is a loving life. The means of mind is the mechanical workings of the brain."

"Science will never prove God is in the heart. How do I find God?"

"Go to your ancestors, enter their rituals, speak with them and hear their stories and music. Myths are stories about reality. To enter mind is to know meaning and to know God."

Radha

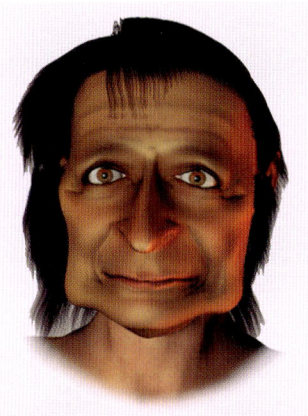

has returned to India where she was born. She cooks for her uncles, aunts and cousins, and illustrates the Hindu myths for a publishing company. She has a lot of free time, which she needs for her devotions and meditations. Often she simply sits by the river bank and goes into a trance.

Her inner life is very rich. She hears voices that allow her to be a channel if she so chooses. Some New Age Western people like to form groups and get all excited by hearing channeling from "Ascended Masters." But Radha knows that the beings that oversee her process are guides, people who have passed over to the other side and are appointed or drawn to help.

For three years, however, Radha was brought into great illusion and delusion by channeling tricksters and mean ghosts. At that time, she had to quit all work, for she was completely wrapped up in their tricks and her energy was drained from her. They tried to kill her and take her soul, but something within her said, "You are who you are and no one can take that from you."

During this dark night of the soul she was awake all night and all day and was delirious much of the time. She did not go to a doctor, as her friends advised, because she knew it was not a medical problem and she feared they would lock her up in a mental institution. Slowly and with determination, by speaking to her Ab day by day, moment by moment, she sought to rectify any injustices she ever did to anyone in any lifetime.

She prayed with all sincerity, "I don't mind dying, but please, dear One Source, release me from any and all aberrations I have ever had, so that I can purify and be free of all interference to my natural emotional and mental state. I am forever dedicated to serving thy highest good in whatever way I can."

Ingalook

has communed with his soul all his life. Being in resonance with Nature on a deep level has enabled him to have stable sanity, but sorrow still comes to him through his empathy with plants, animals and also humans. He has taken an interest in the migrations of various tribes and peoples throughout the ages. He has come to believe that his own Eskimo ancestors came from Asia over the Bering Straight in a time when the Asia and American continents were more connected. So he has come to identify himself with Asian culture as well as Amerindian.

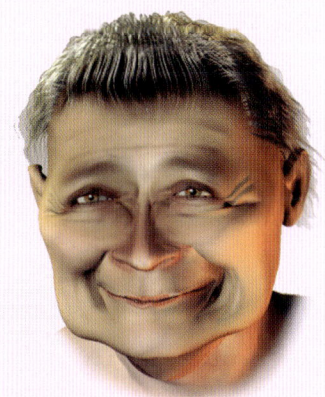

The Taoists of China particularly interest him, for they are one with Nature and even have a shamanic background. Lao Tzu and Chuang Tzu have become like old familiar friends to him. So when he communes with his conscience about anything, he hears his Ab speak through their voices, "Empty yourself of everything. Let the mind rest in peace. The ten thousand things rise and fall while the Self watches their return."

Ingalook grows wise as he feels, intuits and yet remains a detached witness. More and more everyday, his Ab reveals to him how all things arise from the One and return to the One, how the Tao never passes away, and how the conscience is a reflection of the soul.

"I am uncertain of one thing" Ingalook says to his Ab one day as he learns the old ways of hunting and fishing. "How can I be true to myself while harming the fish I spear, the deer I hunt?"

His Ab replies, after many days, "As in the old times, offer prayers for the soul of the fish and deer, ask the Mistress of Animals for permission to hunt before hunting. Remain respectful of all of life."

Ingalook eats only what is necessary for his health and life, always asking permission from the spirit of the animal. He speaks to the particular spirit of the species before plucking a plant. Ingalook is very happy, for people come to him and he lives in harmony with Nature, in harmony with the Tao.

Chapter Twelve:
RECOGNIZING SOUL PURPOSE AMONG THE TWELVE TRIBES

This chapter is an exercise in your honesty and communion with your Ba so that you can realize which soul tribe or tribes you might belong to. Rarely is any person identified with just one of the following archetypes, but you might recognize a few that resonate with you. You are making a synthesis—an integration—of your life with the qualities you recognize. It is alright to identify with one or another tribe even though ultimately one must release all such identification, for each stage of unfoldment brings different experiences and revelations.

In the next twelve pages you will learn more about the twelve archetypes already introduced in Part One. Each archetype has a psychic attractor, a color, and a tone as well as musical interval. These are all functions within the macrocosm as well as within the human as the microcosm. To harmonize heaven (the higher dimensions) and earth (the three dimensions), is to know the functions of the archetypes.

Aberrations, or the misuse of these archetypes is also given. These "fallen" qualities are important to know because you or others you know may be resonating with an archetype, but in a negative or reactive way. Then methods of overcoming the aberrations are given. These are just suggestions. Naturally, the actual work of overcoming aberrations takes consistent, clear practice.

Consciously intending to develop benevolent qualities for each archetype makes a very big difference in your success at overcoming aberrations. Do not give up just because it is difficult to transform what you want to release. To do this work requires consistent dedication. That means unconditional commitment to your soul purpose. And what does that mean? Not giving up with your intention no matter how long it takes or what effort or resources it takes. If there is something conditional about your dedication, your subconscious mind knows it, and it will overpower your intention.

The Ka and Khaibit often collude together to make up an illusion. In their world, it is not an illusion. It is the only reality they know, so they make up a myth about it. But you are intending to be one with your soul, by walking through your shadows and subconscious illusions, to a greater purpose. What is that purpose? That is what you are seeking to know in this chapter.

The pictures are of our twenty-four characters as they go on their journey to find their soul purpose. You may reflect on them as you search your soul. You may resonate more to a picture than to the qualities or vice versa. Just make notes of your thoughts and feelings and more clarity on your soul purpose will come to you.

Vision and Creativity

Point Tribe, tone of C—Fundamental and Octave

To create with the codes and maintain focus, one needs concentration, consistency of the single eye—for shifting angles does not work if the vision is double, triple, or quadruple. To create, to manifest, requires consistent focus and the sign of this focus is creativity and vision. Creativity is a cycle of receptivity, inspiration, imagination, action, manifestation and release that is an unending expression of the love of Prime Source.

The aberration within the archetype of *creating codes* is losing the single clear vision and believing in the illusion of separation. This is the source of multiple realities in various densities of illusion. Stars themselves are seen as centers of fallen light, showing atomic spectra of a dead chemistry by astronomers. Sometimes aberrations of holding a single vision are being a tyrant, that is, over-controlling others because of being fearful of trusting Prime Source. Ego domination over others is one end of the aberrant qualities of this archetype and fear of illusion, (being caught in multiple realities) is the other end.

The way to overcome the illusion of this archetype is by activating the creative force within, embracing all divergent paths with a single vision, and developing the capacity to act and manifest.

Qualities needed to develop are concentration, single-pointed focus, penetrating insight, and seeing multiplicity as unity while honoring apparent differences.

Building Wealth and Structures

Step Tribe, tone of Db—Semitone

People resonating to this archetype are builders, and those who can take step-by-step measures to accomplish something. They are good economists, bankers, money managers as well as potential sculptors, architects, and building contractors. These people are often concerned with material wealth and having possessions. Whether this interest is good or not depends on a balance of incoming wealth and sharing with others.

Our relation to the states of matter is best dealt with as demonstrated by megaliths and pyramids, but also our use of sound and color technologies to balance and heal. Particular types of stones with specific properties enhance the ley line energies, giving people and all of life more *chi* or *prana* (life energy). Without this greater circulation of *chi*, people's consciousness falls and the pyramids and megaliths are seen as places to loot and plunder.

The abuse of this archetype comes from domination of others through economics and building for ego aggrandizement. It also consists of a consciousness of people who continue to mine, disturb the electromagnetic spectrum (The devastating Haarp experiment), create bombs, burn fossil fuels, in essence—disturb all four states of matter. The Step tribe essentially loves the four states of matter and knows how each is vital to life and consciousness. Power points and ley lines are to be revered and kept clear.

Qualities to develop with this archetype are gently holding, building, accumulating, and attracting beauty and values for the good of the whole.

Distribution and Communication

Branch Tribe, tone of D—Wholetone

The way you communicate is a sign of your cultivation, and creativity is the root code of culture. To recognize what your inspiration is and then to take action on it is to be a part of the tree of knowledge. To embody your soul purpose is to be a part of the tree of life.

The people resonating to this archetype see the hierarchy in Nature and spirit and do not confuse it with political or power hierarchies, which may abuse power. These people are concerned with community and how one aspect relates to another in a spiritual, as well as a grounded, sense. Real communicators want to understand the laws and principles of the universe and to relate only the truth to others.

Aberrations of this archetype are miscommunication, bias in media or journalism, and a confusion of tongues, symbolized by the Tower of Babel. Behind these aberrations are fear, judgement and projection. Be aware how fear—of being judged and fear that there is no order to the universe—is disempowering.

Culture heros are higher dimensional contributors to this archetype. Culture heros reach out and create tools for all of humanity to use in order to lead them back to source. This is to know that the tree of life is upside down to the tree of knowledge. The tree of life has its roots in heaven, in higher dimensions. Rely on laws, principles and archetypes and the love of God. Then the fruits of the earth will unfold.

Qualities needed to strengthen this archetype: to know one's soul purpose is to align with God first, to find the ways to distribute to the community and actualize a fruitful life together.

Generating and Managing Energy

Spiral Tribe, tone of E♭—Minor Third

People strongly influenced by this archetype are concerned with being able to generate energy for themselves and others. Therefore, their health and desires are important. Desire is the root of generating energy flow, including money, health, and sexuality.

In a balanced way, these people can generate funds, energy, and grants for others as well as themselves. People managing trade, economics, and exchange systems may be of this type. Energy and economics are primary here.

Aberrations of this archetype may manifest as being a "workaholic," that is, being driven. They may go with the energy of a gang, clan or tribe. There is a feeling of lack and powerlessness, so they go for money-energy and power. Feeling lack, they seek to hoard or overpower others. Their own desires are primary to them.

How can one rectify the "not enough" syndrome? Cease grasping for results. Let go of expectations. Open to the energy of the **Living Now**. Be open to synchronous experience awareness. Receive every event in life as nurturance. Pray to be connected to source and source of source. Create. Allow the unknown to be a presence in day-to-day life. Enjoy the ride. Behold energy everywhere. Give thanks to your mother. Give thanks to Mother Earth and Mother Galaxy. Give thanks to the Nurturing Goddess.

Qualities to develop for the embodiment of the Spiral tribe are spontaneity, living in the now, following one's joy.

Radiant Harmony and Dynamic Peace

Radial Tribe, tone of E—Major Third

Meaning is found when heart and mind are united. Positive signs of this archetype are those who want to maintain the codes of their own value system, such as myths, chants, and traditional art. When in harmony with your soul, true values are felt by your cells. In a mythical sense, cells radiate harmony from the Love-Light broadcast from the heart of the Sphinx. For she receives the songs of the God of Light, playing the harmonics of the Hyos Ha Koidesh, whose sacred geometry holds the polarity of the oscillating universe.

When the mind is not one with the heart, the Love-Light from the DNA in your cells is not activated fully. Then the mystery of the Sphinx as living love is not revealed to humans. Signs are torment, and despair. The root of aberrations of this archetype are despair, lack of trust, and a sense of meaninglessness.

The way to find dynamic peace, one with Archangel Gabriel, is to open the mind to the heart and to open the heart to the One Mind of Prime Source/Creatrix. The torment and conflict issues from their apparent severance and a lack of trust and realization that heart and mind are one.

Qualities needed to open the mystery of this archetype are trust, openness and love. Then the beautiful Light of the Hyos Ha Koidesh and Gabriel will shine through your own heart, dispelling fear, torment, and despair.

Right Use of Life-Substance

Loop Tribe, tone of F—Perfect Fourth

The ecosystem is not only a food chain, but is a delicate interaction and respect for plants and animals and their mutual coexistence. All beings have souls, and requesting permission to eat of a plant, and gratitude for all animals, is a way of allowing the transformation of substance to be a sacred act.

The aberration on earth, of the *transform substance* archetype is the slaughter of plants and animals for their wood, pelts, antlers, hides and meat. This abuse stems from a lack of appreciation for the soul and essence of plants and animals and lack of awareness of the transience of all of life. The human is one with plants and animals, and is dependent externally for oxygenated air and food from plants. We are also cellulary one with plants and animals.

Ignorance on human's part is rooted in an insensitivity and lack of love for one's own existence. Appreciation each moment for the vitality of life and a whole-hearted love for all sentience enables one to release attachment and let go of such protective coatings as overeating, waste of paper and wood products, and killing animals for meat and hide without respect of their essence.

Qualities to develop to embody this archetype are transformative power, honor and respect, and sacrifice in the sense of "making sacred."

Balance and Standing Upright

Column Tribe, tone of F#—Tritone

To create connection is to balance extremes and to realize how justice naturally comes about when one is not attached to specific results, such as making a lot of money from a lumber business. Plants are living sentient beings and they create oxygen for animals to breathe, hold soil in place and fertilize soils, provide shade and balance water on earth, and they are sensitive, aware, feeling vital beings. Plants were created by Prime Source from pure Mind, the Hashmalim and justice. They assist humans in resurrection by demonstrating how to be receptive to light, and by breaking apart rock to absorb minerals. It is a slow and steady, receptive and growing path to be a plant.

The aberration of the *create connection* archetype is a posturing forward or back, not being able to stand on one's own feet and stand up for what one believes. This includes aggression on trees, forests—all of plant life. To stand up straight is to balance extremes and to integrate spirit and matter through a detached acceptance. One's spine is an axis of beliefs. When rectifying beliefs based on receptivity to spirit, then one stands up naturally. The natural curvature of the spine is neither bent forward nor back, but is an S curve.

Qualities to develop are detachment, balance and steadiness. Standing up for what one believes is essential to embody this archetype. Standing up to and speaking about injustices is also part of this archetypal quality.

Power and Health

Wave Tribe, tone of G—Perfect Fifth

The spiritual water above the Cherubim is the source of sexuality as spiritual love. When fear arises, it is a sign than sexuality and spiritual love are severed. The desire to kill that which one fears stems from this division. The power-monger is fearful because of unfulfilled desires. The root of all healing is in reuniting sexual and spiritual love and using power for the benefit of the whole.

The twenty four wings of the Cherubim vibrate in happiness when the animal nature transforms fear into love that can celebrate sexuality as purity. The beautiful courtship dances of animals are an expression of the healing spiritual water above. All aspects of the animal rejoice in the moments of courtship where a consummation of "above" and "below" is fulfilled. The dragons are protectors of the treasure house of vibrations that issue forth from the *Logos* as the voice of Prime Source/Creatrix.

Qualities needed for healing the separation of sexual and spiritual love, and consequently all wounds, are integrity, speaking the truth of one's feelings, and allowing sexuality to be a natural process of surrendering to God within one's beloved.

Transformation toward Divinity

Diamond Tribe, tone of Ab—Minor Sixth

People strongly influenced by this archetype seek dynamic Oneness, wholeness and behold everything as part of a unity. They often are meditators and live in transcendent states. The soul always has the choice or capacity to align with pure spirit. Purpose stems from alignment of soul with Prime Source. Then one can feel the vibrations of the Seraphim and move in a direction of love and peace. The human ultimately has no choice but to align soul, mind, and body with pure spirit. The human task is to integrate the plant, animal, mineral, planetary, stellar, galactic, atomic, subatomic, cellular, ecological, and cultural realms into one embodiment and allow wisdom and love to guide all relations. Then the presence of the human before Prime Source announces the harmonic fulfillment of all orders of being.

Aberrations are "space-cases," not being grounded or fully in the body. But then this type may also seek to manipulate out of despair. This leads to nihilism, a destructive state of consciousness where everything seems pointless. Despair's root is the lack of trust and the refusal to surrender to Prime Source. The corruption of the soul, relating to this archetype, is perhaps the most insidious of all corruptions, for when the soul is dragged by the fears of the desire-body into grasping, reaction, sexual violence, theft, corporate and political manipulation of the masses, and all the corruptions discussed in previous archetypes, the soul is in despair.

Qualities to develop to embody this archetype are love and trust of Prime Source, surrender to truth, love and beauty, and consideration of the whole of a given situation.

Patience and Work

Sphere Tribe, tone of A—Major Sixth

People resonating to this archetype are often concerned with survival and may indeed be in poverty and struggling. Or they may have worked through a fear of lack and provide a protected environment for others, such as shelters, homes for orphans, food and blankets for the needy. These people may also be creative with metal, clay, rocks, gems and be able to generate money and/or goods from their patient labors. Atomic physicists or people interested in how creation builds from simple energies may also be one with this archetype. Hard-working people who have a clear aim and consistent ability to work towards it have qualities of the Sphere tribe.

The negative aspect of this archetype is being fearful of lack and hoarding. To steal, hoard, mine, become controlling and miserly of minerals and money is to abuse the spiritual earth—which is a force that cannot be corrupted. The abuse bounces back to the offenders. Miserliness becomes need and comes from need. Mining is a disease that affects the offender's bones. Sodium, silicon, carbon, nitrogen, chlorine and neon are all harmonics of the spiritual earth that have specific numbers, correlating to the angles of atoms. The Elim order the harmonic numbers and thereby the atoms are created.

Qualities needed to be at one with the Sphere tribe are patience, consistency, and all-embracing consciousness. Curiosity and firm values are needed in this archetype.

Networking and Integration

Grid Tribe, tone of B♭—Minor Seventh

This archetype reveals people concerned with maintaining relationships—networkers, and people wanting community wholeness. Collective consciousness is an awakening of other's values and care. Sometimes aspects of government are put into play through this archetype.

Aberrations are sabotaging group consciousness through a frustration of not fitting in. Hackers of the world wide web are of this type. Governmental control through mind, hypnosis, trance, including use of media, when not of good motive for the whole, are aberrations of this archetype.

To reach this archetype is to know the nine muses of inspiration, and to know how to integrate and weave together disparate threads of thought. What thoughts have gone astray or dissipate energy? What thoughts distract from your soul purpose? The integrity of one's being is inherent in soul. Every soul is a whole and a part of the Throne of God.

It is through the trinity of science, arts and spirituality that one answer is found: Science—observation, experiment, and contemplation; Arts—sound, color/form, and movement; Spirituality—myth, ritual, and scriptures.

Grids are systems of consciousness, interconnecting realms and dimensions. Qualities to cultivate are discernment and integration, weaving and evaluating, measuring and fitting.

Delightful Uncertainty

Unpredictable Tribe, tone of B—Major Seventh

People resonating with this archetype are often mavericks and give up wanting to fit in. Rebels and creative people move on this path, for society needs fresh ideas, critics of the status quo, and open possibilities. Creativity and destruction are close twins, for de-structuring is essential for renewal. The beneficent enactors of this archetype flow to and from the source with ease and delightful uncertainty. One cannot cling to anything in this function, but must surrender to each moment in open trust.

Uncertainty may also be expressed as mystery, the unknown and the unknowable. With this archetype one reaches to the extremes of both hell and heavenly realms—dimensions below three and above three. Ultimately, the subatomic realm is rooted in the Void, called the vacuum by physicists. The Void, which is actualy a plenum or fullness, is the ground of Prime Source.

When applied from a motive of hate, anger, and fear, this archetype leads only to nihilism, which is the waste-dump of the universe. Terrorism is the social invention that plays negatively upon this function. Mystics also live on the path of the receptive force. One criteria for being a mystic is going through a dark night of the soul. Mystics and terrorists may be positive and negative extreme expressions of the same archetype. What do they have in common? Uncertainty. The mystic intends the will of God and the terrorist intends self-will or the will of his/her rebel group.

Qualities needed to embody this archetype are trust, receptivity, openness to uncertainty and feeling one with the Void-Plenum.

Chapter Thirteen:
LIVING SOUL PURPOSE

Sixth Initiation: The BA or Soul

The Ba resides within your Sahu, the most creative and integrative spiritual body, one with Prime Source. So knowing your Ba is a paramount process along the way of integrating all Nine Bodies. You had a cursory practise of knowing your soul purpose in the last chapter. But now, resonating more to your Khaibit and Ab, (shadow and conscience), you are in a better position to truly know you Ba.

Our characters have integrated two or more archetypes in the sixth initiation, which is key to discovering more about soul purpose. What this really means is that you know your soul and align all your lower bodies with soul purpose rather than the other way around. To know your Ba is to be sensitive to the deepest intuition and knowing and trust yourself. This is a practice of knowing the Ba that can move through all obstacles in life. Your soul purpose is not really likely to be conventional, status quo "adult" behavior. It is a unique calling that only you can respond to. The call is from your Ba.

The Ba may be unique, but it is also one with a high dimensional group soul. If more people are honest about their shadows and commune with their conscience, then it will be easier to recognize other people who are part of your soul group. This is not in order to make a clan, or some group separate from the whole; but rather to see how a given archetypal quality contributes to the whole. Wherever there is separatism or elitism, whether for good or ill, it is not recognizing its part in the whole.

The symbols in this section combine two or more archetypes into one symbol. Symbols are doorways to the higher dimensions, to the invisible world. Trusting that there are higher dimensional worlds is part of the process. This is not foolish hope, but is based on direct experience that you know inwardly from your initiations.

Exercise

Pay attention to the qualities of each symbol. Write down what they mean to you. Find or create other symbols that you feel attracted to. What psychic attractors do they combine?

As you go through this next chapter, reflect on the characters, but also on why the characters resonate to the symbols given. The pictures of each character's Ba is shown with wings. This is symbolic of the soul being able to take flight. When it is attached to the body, the lower self is aligned with the soul. If the wings are off in space, the Ba is waiting until the personality is willing to align with it. All the characters in the following pages have their wings attached, because they are undergoing a dedication ceremony on the invisible planes, that aligns all aspects of them with their soul.

Living from soul purpose brings intense intrinsic joy and that is the intention of this chapter.

Ariel's

life is as intense as ever, but she is discovering the divinity in her vision. She is seeing with an inner eye and beginning to paint mystical landscapes and visions of celestial spaces.

During the ceremony the sixth initiation, Ariel learned what her dedication is:

"I am dedicated to being a divine eye, to bring forth beauty from the Fountain of Truth."

She hears a voice, "The eye is both bindu (point) and sphere, both spiral and vesica. You are to marry concentration with grounded substance, to integrate generating energy flow with new birth." It is Isis speaking in a dream.

Shawn

goes for a walk in the desert by himself. The tangles of his conscious, subconscious and unconscious aspects become more untangled, the more he walks and observes Nature.

Coming back to his house, he goes immediately to his harp and begins playing. "I am the wind, I am the hawk, I am the cactus flower along the path of life. I am the sun, I am the love in the middle of the moon." As he sings the song over and over in musical variations, he comes into peace and stillness. His Ba inside of him declares, "I will be who I am, regardless of what others think. I am one with the sun and moon." He dips into sleep for just half an hour and when he awakes, he says to himself "I now know my dedication for our ceremony: I am both seed and receptacle and accept myself as I am: androgynous."

Frank

seeks clarity on his soul purpose through sacred geometry. His symbol is the step and grid combined.

Now that Frank has begun to cease being a workaholic, he relaxes into communion with both his Ab and Ba through his heart. His heart and mind are becoming one, not only in potential, but in action. He has started a new business of designing buildings for others and letting the labor be done by others. For he has already established his ability to do actual physical work. At night, his Ba speaks to him, "You are inherently a designer, using harmonic proportions. The universe itself is based on such principles. Love is the first principle and harmony is the second. When you open your heart, harmony will be there also."

Elizabeth

realizes she has boxed herself in, and yet boxes and containers, limits and proportions are important in her ability to organize.

Elizabeth has become very well-liked and appreciated at the school in the library, for she managed to not reject herself when the teachers criticized her.

"I am as I am," she says to herself. "I am taking steps to reorder my life."

When she grows quiet, even in the midst of the activity in the library, she looks at the children and hears her soul speak, "I am loved, for I am love. I am learning to love more by ceasing to attach to people and activities I desire. I am more and more accepting of myself as I am."

Karen

truly begins to feel to strength that is beyond her business.

She searches her soul for the purpose that she can trust to be fulfilling. She has to go beyond what she is doing to find being at her very foundations.

"I am the nourished and nourishing. I am rooted in God and branch out from my soul. I am strong and fulfilled. My strength and wholeness come from a source beyond my apparent existence." Tears of gratitude come to her eyes.

Then she notices that she no longer feels overwhelmed, for she is actually strong in herself and aligned with her soul purpose.

Morgan

has changed from warrior to an opener of a new way.

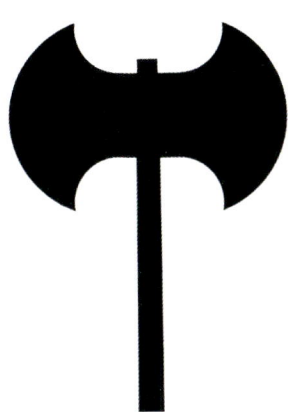

"This feels better" Morgan declares to himself. "The double-headed axe is both straight and curved, both masculine and feminine, both outer and inner." He finds himself awkward at first, speaking to people with respect instead of his former impatience and control.

In the Ba initiation ceremony at night, even though he is unconscious of it, he vows: "I am both sharp and soft. I dedicate myself to entering into everything I invent, appreciating all the patterns, atoms, branches, hinges, and substance that goes into each one. I am not apart from anything, and my inventions are God's to use as he-she will."

Ricardo

   is letting go of prejudice and a feeling of abandonment.

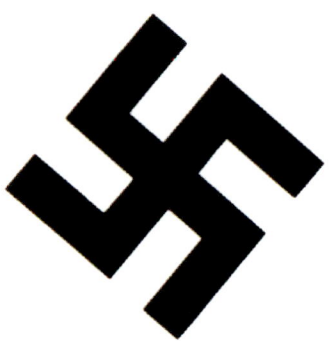

   Ricardo has primordial roots in Middle and South America, where the swastika symbol was used and understood to be the One Divine Source that turns all things. As Ricardo walks in the night, he looks up at the stars and says to himself, "The Pole Star is the center of a swastika with others stars rotating around it."

   Ricardo speaks within as to his soul, "I have Source within me, as do all beings. I release all sense of being unsupported, abandoned and let go of wanting others to depend on me. I dedicate myself to turning the wheel of the law from Source within myself."

Jennifer

now dances at the sea shore, across streams, in the meadows and forests. Her swirls and twirls arch back upon themselves in spirals and spins that open up her energy channels.

Jennifer is finding her soul purpose in generating subtle energy for her own life and for others. More and more young people, not only learn dancing from her, but like to hang around her. She tells stories, and mimics the characters she depicts. Her Ba says to her, "Open up and reveal your wildness. They already know of your discipline and steadiness."

Jennifer becomes the old witch, the young virgin, and the desirous young man, imitating each one in turn and making the children laugh and giggle with delight.

Serafina

loves flowers, color, light, and beauty. She has decided that it no longer serves her to do what others want her to do, but to listen to her soul.

Serafina's Ba is one with her every brush-stroke as she paints, for her soul purpose is to reveal the oneness of light and color throughout all realms. On one of her watercolor expeditions she makes a dedication that wells up from her heart: "I trust I am supported as I respond to my calling to reveal the beauty of spirit in Nature day by day, moment by moment. Beauty is within me, around me and all through me as it is all through the world."

Francis

finds the pentagram within his own heart, and is finding a balance between five ways.

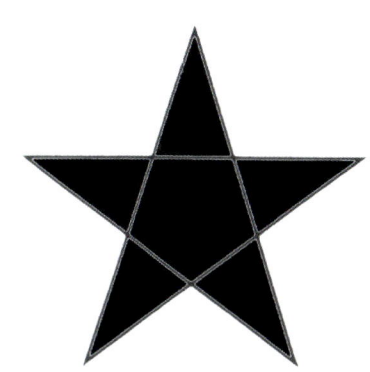

Francis's wildness is still present, but is now refined into the most paradoxical poetry of the heart. He finds himself in love with everything and everyone. He makes a clear dedication to his soul: "I open my heart to the truth at all times. I radiate love at all times. I am one with God, earth, culture and family. Help me be constant in fulfilling my intention."

"Gold, yellow, lambs, limbs, lumber, rumble, old folds burn through the deep," he mumbles to himself as he wanders through the world.

Francesca

reaches to heaven to find the center of all crossroads.

Francesca declares, "I dedicate myself to living as the plants do: with perfect equanimity, feeling loved, and opening to the unity of all divisions. I can be discerning without making judgements about others or myself. Everyday I am feeling more and more supported. I trust the divine center within me."

Francesca goes into the stillpoint where all polarities cease. She sighs a deep sigh, as she continues to walk and observe Nature in the desert.

Ramon

receives, as his symbol, the infinity sign representing his ability to move from inside to outside and from outside to inside: from receptivity to activity and back again.

Ramon's Ba is very penetrating and powerful. Ramon is more able to commune with his soul and then direct a film from the inside out. He is also more receptive to the essential being of his actors are and who his camera and sound crew are.

He makes a prayer: "I ask that the truth and beauty of Latino peoples be revealed through me. Let me show our struggle against being victims without being victims. I ask for help in presenting reality as a statement of fact, without reaction of anger, hatred, or revenge."

Dolores

listens intently now and feels her own power, for she has been bestowed with an Ankh from Isis on the inner planes.

Dolores makes a renewed dedication of her soul: " I trust the universe for complete support and I support others whenever it is easy and natural for me to do so."

She communes with her Ba when she goes into the stillness before sleeping, sometimes in prayer, sometimes in her own statement of intention: "I am grateful for life; I am grateful for seeing how to transform victimhood into empowerment. I ask only for greater and greater clearing of any resistances I may have to being who I am."

Horus

has received the symbol of the Djed pillar, which is a sign of resurrection and regeneration.

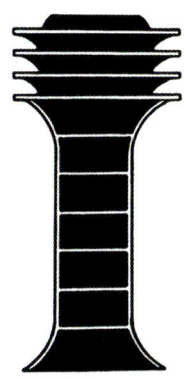

Horus is genuinely dedicated to uprightness. He has searched many parts of the world for methods of mediation and justice, and is coming to prefer a mediation community counsel, but this is only if there are elders or wise people who can form such a counsel.

He prays now for insight about how to create such a counsel in his own community: "I am dedicated to finding the most equitable way of helping people in dispute see the other's point of view."

Ratta

receives the thunderbolt symbol because she is so charged and able to wield her power in various directions.

Ratta's soul seeks to know the unknown, the mysterious—the deeps of the human psyche. After her Hawaiian adventure, she goes many places where so-called "primitive" peoples live: She met with the aborigines of Australia and the Maoris of New Zealand. She enters their ceremonies with the same dedication: "I am here to transmit the power of the Divine Source. I have no limits and yet I live on earth with humble awe of each person, plant and stone. Help me live true to myself, true to these people, true to the Great Spirit of All."

David

receives the Tai Chi (yin-yang) symbol because he is always balancing his masculine and feminine sides.

David's soul purpose is to be true to his innate sense of joy and beauty, as well as vitality and strength. His intensity is difficult to manage, but he is learning the chords of music through patterns rather than written music and is able to create dynamic music that is both tender and forceful. He is passionate and lives in a loving force-field as long as he is creating. He makes a dedication: "I live in accordance with the rhythms, tones, and pulses that move through me, and that are harmonious with my heart-mind."

Humphrey

receives the bindu-point inside the union of heaven and earth.

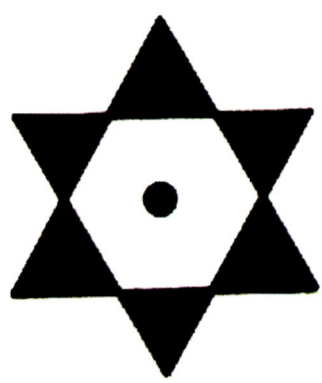

Humphrey knows the inner spaces of deep contemplation. He is disciplined in meditation and knows core truths. His question is, "Is the world ready for my insights?"

He does not applaud himself in front of others. He has been very reclusive up to now. But his Ba, his soul, is calling him to speak, write, publish, and share. He says, "I am dedicated to standing in the center of the Void and speaking about the relation of inner to outer and how all is a gift to be transformed and returned to Source."

soul has the scarab-resurrection symbol, for she is a soul who moves beyond the status quo.

Clare has found happiness within herself. The relationship of God to Nature through the human is clearly a cultural phenomenon that depends upon human wisdom, but also human daring, courage, and openness to transformation.

She makes a dedication: "I declare myself an agent and midwife to death and resurrection. Without de structuring, there can be no new structuring. My soul knows the truths of the ages and I will not hesitate to share the perennial wisdom wherever there is interest."

144

Shobak Shu

receives the triple spiral as a symbol, for his soul is ancient and yet he creates methods and ritual anew.

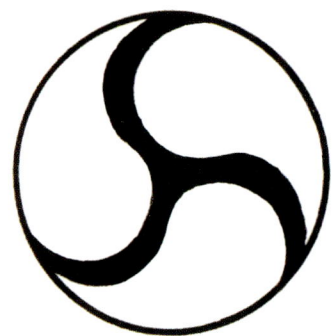

Shobak Shu speaks to his soul through his drum. More and more he is asked to offer a shamanic journey, to do healings, and retrieve souls even from white people. Every time he serves in this way, he speaks to his Ba, his soul: "Please let me be an agent of love and truth for my brother and sister human beings here. They have suffered enough. It is time to reveal to them their own healing way. I offer this work to the Supreme One. "

Shobak Shu's shamanic work spreads and he now has sincere students.

Janet

has become a more and more clear vessel. The grail symbol is written within her heart.

Janet's soul is a clear vessel, a grail, and she is learning to align with it day by day. This takes persistent practise, but she has made an unconditional commitment to her own soul. She speaks to her Ba as she enters a clear, high mountain range, "I am dedicated to being true to my soul, known within my own heart, no matter what happens outwardly in my family, my work or in the world. Everyday I correct myself if I fall back to making decisions based on pleasing others."

Joe

receives the circles in grid symbol that reverses its polarity. He is finding that what is black and white is reversible and temporary, but there is something invisible within that makes it work.

Joe knows in his soul how the web of life is woven. His research mind finds fulfillment in being mind to mind with students. He is beginning to find the center of polarities and to live with trust. The myths of his ancestors refer to a creator. As he explores the stories of diverse African tribes; they all have creators who cannot be understood with the small mind. "I am dedicated to living in consciousness of the One Mind that lives in all minds. Help me see, feel and know God within each soul."

Wadabu

recieves the Fleur d' Lis as a symbol because she balances polarities with humour and grace.

The soul of Wabadu is very ancient and full of courage and loving kindness. She realizes, though, that working with so many hurt and angry people of diverse races, is tiring if she doesn't align all of her personality with her Ba, her soul.

During one of the ceremonies in Africa she says, "I am dedicated to being true to my soul and helping everyone I can when I am balanced and stable. I pray to be thus empowered. I am love. I am truth. I am goodness."

Ingalook

opens his heart to everyone, so he has received the multiple heart symbol.

Feeling centered and peaceful, Ingalook welcomes anyone who comes to his small cabin in the north. He still travels as a healer and shaman, so he meets many new people. He serves them tea and food and offers them shelter if he has it available. Every morning and every night he offers a dedication: "I surrender to the One and find the One in all beings. The invisible and intangible source is the essence of love. Help me be love and totally love."

Radha

receives the AUM symbol as the highest form of vibration that penetrates to the One through the Void. She has become fearless through her dark night of the soul.

Radha stands on the bank of the sea and chants mantras and songs to God. Her devotion increases her vital energy, for she knows it is not hers, but is a gift. So when she cooks for her relatives, she gives good vibrations to the food, and everyone around is becoming healthier and happier. She says to her soul at night, "I am dedicated to being one with thee as you are dedicated to the one God. May all beings be happy."

On the inner planes our twenty-four characters meet for a soul (Ba) initiation one night. They each inwardly make dedications that night, in accordance with their understanding of their soul purpose. They are shown here with robes of two or more patterns and colors, in accordance with their soul evolution.

Summary of the Nine Egyptian Light Bodies

The nine bodies of the Egyptians are intermediary between the physical and spiritual worlds, between the Void and the harmonic order of angels and light councils. The three spiritual bodies of the Sekhem, Sahu and Khu are the most subtle of all the nine bodies. But one cannot identify with or embody these spiritual bodies without extreme work on the lower bodies. Then passion can transform into compassion. Therefore, what follows is a brief review of the bodies.

The psychic bodies of the Khaibit, Ab and Ba play a powerful role in human lives in the transformation of passion into compassion. The Ka is a body image of the denser physical body and it has symbolic representation of an imaginal realm which it may distort. The Khaibit is more subtle than the Ka, but it is unconscious or remembered only in trance states. The Khaibit weaves a mythic reality from both the personal and collective memory of experiences. The dark mysterious world of the Khaibit is as real or objective as the physical body, and must be reckoned with.

The Ab, as the conscience, can rectify the Khaibit's creative myth in moments of extreme honesty, which inevitably is humbling. Forgiveness pours forth from the Ab, which is a reflection of the Ba, the imperishable soul. These moments of honest insight, and self-confession, transform and transmute the Khaibit's reality, so that a more clear reality is seen.

The Ka or body image is influenced by the Khaibit's myth and psychology, and the Khaibit is influenced by the Ab, who only asks, "What is true?" The physical bodies then have disease or health, accidents or ease and harmony, based on the psycho-mental bodies of the so-called imaginal realm.

The Spiritual Bodies

The Sekhem is a spiritual body that links body and spirit through consciousness. The Sekhem transmits the Sa or life-force that highly evolved beings draw upon to become immortals. The "backward-flowing circulation of the Light" of the Chinese, the *kundalini* rising up the *sushumna* of Yoga, the becoming one with the *Logos* of John's *Revelation*, are all the self-luminous rebirth of eternal light. The birth of Christos is what Jeshua meant by saying, "I am the Light of the World; he who follows me will walk in darkness, but will have the Light of Life." (John 8.12)

Assimilation of Sa or life-force by the Sekhem and its transmission up the central subtle canal to what the yogis call the brahmarandhra at the sagittal suture of the head, is a key to activating the spiritual body of the Sahu, which is a magical-spiritual body. Access to the Sahu requires long and arduous inner work. So-called primitive societies seek to access it by extreme rituals, trials and potential death ceremonies. The aspirant may briefly experience the Sahu in radical rituals, but rarely is there sustained integration of this spiritual body. Artists sometimes tap into the Sahu if the personality is subdued and humbled, and the creative fountain is activated. The Sahu can work magic for good or ill. The Ba (soul) resides in the Sahu and thereby can have creative and magical experiences.

The Khu, the highest spiritual body, is totally one with Prime Source and cannot be swayed by any personal agendas. The Khu resonates on the higher dimensions where the gods, goddesses, angelic orders and light councils reside. The Khu is filled with light codes or universal symbols that can be seen when resonating on the Khu's level of reality. The Khu penetrates all other light bodies.

Chapter Fourteen:

SEVENTH INITIATION—The SEKHEM,
YOUR VITAL ENERGY and KUNDALINI POWER

Being caught in duality rebounds upon the Sekhem body as the two side channels are a positive and negative polarity. To come fully into the Sekhem body is to allow the kundalini to rise up the central channel. As you have more experiences in life, and also discern the meaning of life through difficult and easy, light and dark, painful and joyful experience, you come into greater understanding that either extreme is not the truth. So how do you access your Sekhem, your kundalini energy, to allow it to pass up into the central channel?

This is to ask, how do you find the stillpoint amidst all extremes, the neutral point amidst polarities? How do you detach from identifying with good over bad or bad over good? How do you compassionately witness yourself having dualistic experiences and yet not attaching to them?

There are two main resistances to becoming who you really are: being overly distracted (busy, busy activities) and being overly dull and unconscious (excessive sleep, torpor, drunkenness, drugs, escapism). To access your kundalini power is to surrender all ego attachment to anything, which is a rare event in human life. The twenty-four characters revealed in this book all have different experiences, different souls and different wisdoms, but they share the fact that it is impossible to access consistent balanced kundalini power while being fearful or attached.

Desire and fear are the root of the dualities that keep us in bondage, but we needn't call them "evil" or make judgement on these experiences at all. Just experience and witness, experience and witness until insight comes on how to be still and know that I AM.

Exercise

Recall an experience in which you felt so much desire that you thought you couldn't live without the person or object you desired. Observe what happened to the object or person and observe what happened to your desire.

Recall an experience in which you were deeply frightened to an extreme degree. It might be some kind of attack, visible or invisible, or when you thought you were going to die, or when you felt you might lose your lover. Now recall what happened as you came through that fear. Perhaps you came through only a part of it, and part of it is still deep within your psyche, yet to be cleared. Allow yourself to delve into these memories and these states of feeling.

Now as you recall experiences of both desire and fear, have compassion for yourself, know that it will change, that all desires and fears pass away. What remains? Be still and know your own being.

CADUCEUS

The one symbol for the Sekhem is the Caduceus. It has two serpents (waves) weaving around a central column with a pine cone on top (representing the pineal gland and the crown chakra). The pine cone is somewhat of a sphere with interlacing spirals.

Ariel's Sekhem

is now rooted deep in the earth, enabling her to reach higher in her consciousness.

Shawn's Sekhem

is becoming radiant like the sky. The polarities are still real, but the soul is receptive to stillness.

Elizabeth's Sekhem

is off center, but luminous, rising into the head, and lights up dark skies.

Frank's Sekhem

is broad and steady, grounded deep in the earth and slowly rising.

Karen's Sekhem

is warm and yet highly spiritual, for dual experiences are being refined through her detachment.

Morgan's Sekhem

shows some detachment and heart-centering, but is struggling still amidst realms of change.

Jennifer's Sekhem

shows more and more simple caring and yet longing for release.

Ricardo's Sekhem

has risen to ultra states of consciousness and is about to surrender totally.

Serafina's Sekhem

is clear and full of longing, but some hidden desires keep her in duality.

Francis' Sekhem

is grounded, vibrating and rising to flood his whole body.

Francesca's Sekhem

is vibrating from multiple experiences that reach for meaning.

Ramon's Sekhem

is grounded in real experiences and is polarized between above and below, which are becoming reconciled.

Dolores's Sekhem

is grounded, reaches for the stars, but needs clearing in the heart.

Horus' Sekhem

shows profound experiences of duality that are witnessed in stillness and balance.

Ratta's Sekhem

is clear except for deep desires still hidden in the unconscious.

David's Sekhem

shows brilliance and secret fears that are held in check by extreme aspirations.

Clare's Sekhem

shows profound experience and brilliant consciousness polarized.

Humphrey's Sekhem

is even and clearing the more he surrenders to God.

Janet's Sekhem

is rising out of difficult experiences that she has neutralized.

Shobak Shu's Sekhem

is glowing at the base and crown and runs all through when he releases all desires.

Wabdu's Sekhem

is complexly woven of obtuse experiences that are being neutralized.

Joe's Sekhem

is spacious and broad, grounded and reaching beyond the stars.

Radha's Sekhem

is vibrating all through with subtle weavings that will soon shoot into the beyond.

Ingalook's Sekhem

penetrates the atmospheres of distant spheres through adhering to the One.

159

Chapter Fifteen:
HOW IS YOUR TOTAL SPIRITUAL INTEGRATION?

EIGHTH INITIATION—The SAHU

Using supreme symbols—the Shri Yantra, the Wheel of the Law, the Step, the Tree of Life, the Weave—the Ba finds its direction within a greater whole of a higher dimensional world. Your specific symbols, tones, patterns, colors are all inherent within the greater whole. In this initiation you need to find what in your life you are integrating, or that your soul wants to integrate.

Here, the robes integrate three or more patterns and begin to scintillate with light codes in greater integration.

1) Wheel: Francis, Shawn and Ratta
2) Grid: Joe, Clare, Karen
3) Loopl: Francesca, Elizabeth, David
4) Tree of Life: Morgan, Dolores, Jennifer
5) Flow: Ingalook, Ricardo, Serafina
6) Circles/Flower of Life: Horus, Wabadu, Janet
7) Amerindian Step: Frank, Radha, Ramon
8) Shri Yantra: Humphrey, Shobak Shu and Ariel

Any trials in the sixth initiation are likely between your Ba and Khaibit, but if the identity has been with the lower bodies, then there may be dissipation and lack of Sekhem regenerating, so the Ka and Sahu bodies may be depleted also. Examine yourself for any discrepancy between your inner intent and outer life. The Sahu works through the art of life. This means that there is resonance between consciousness, soul purpose, codes and how one creates and manifests in the outer world.

The Sahu is an inner state of consciousness that knows what it knows and moves into crafting, shaping, that is, manifesting what it knows. Inspiration is paramount here, but so is the ability to take action.

Exercise

Make a mandala of your life by first creating a graph that outlines the physical, emotional, mental and spiritual aspects of your life, crossed with time periods of about five years. Find the low points, the peaks, the places and times of neutrality. Find when you had all four aspects of your life more or less integrated.

Second get a large sheet of paper (or other media) and make a great circle. Within the circle, make four divisions, for example north, south, east and west. Let north indicate symbolically times of receptivity in voidness. This could mean spiritual insight or inspiration. In the east, remember times in your life when you had a clear vision, perhaps started a new project, communicated a true idea you had or have. In the south, look at your life in terms of manifestation. What have you actually accomplished, fulfilled, brought to fruition? In the west, indicate times in your life when you've let go of something. This was a time of release, death, disorientation and even confusion.

You might make the mandala with the earlier years being on the inside and the recent years on the outside, using a great spiral. Draw symbols and images of low and peak times in each area.

Meditate on your mandala and observe cycles, patterns that may be positive or negative. What do you want to change?

Now make a mandala of how you want to integrate in the future.

THE WHEEL OF THE LAW

Francis, Shawn and Ratta have moved in diverse ways into the symbol of the Wheel, which integrates the point, radial, and circle. What they now have in common is intense focus that moves out into the world.

GEODESIC SPHERE

Clare, Joe, and Karen are ecstatically integrating the grid, circle, and diamond. This profound integration is vast, cosmic, and transformative, helping in maintaining relationships, or connections between all beings.

THE INTERWOVEN KNOT

Francesca, Elizabeth, and David integrate the loop, the spiral and circle by giving honest feedback, generating energy for beneficial purposes to the global community, and creating funds for wholesome causes.

THE TREE OF LIFE

Dolores, Morgan, and Jennifer work through the tree of life symbol. Each in their own way aligns with the central axis of the universe asking what is true. The branches spin energy flow into the community.

CHAOTIC FLOW

Ingalook, Ricardo, and Serafina are on the edge of mystery and unpredictability. They wing it in the world by riding the currents of energy through spirals, waves and diffusion. Their certitude is all within.

THE FLOWER OF LIFE AND DIAMOND

Horus, Wabadu, and Janet integrate by means of the circled grid, which forms diamonds and points. They are all involved with maintaining connections through clear communication and self-transformation.

THE STEPPED PYRMID

Frank, Radha, and Ramon are all building foundations and platforms for invocation, prayer, and cosmic attunement. Deep meditation is the basis for substantial foundations for new culture-making

SHRI YANTRA

Humphrey, Ariel, and Shobak Shu are divinely inspired to make prayers and offerings in many places. In various ways, they travel, write, create art, and heal by using the divine codes of the point, circle and diamond.

Chapter Sixteen:
THE NINTH INITIATION—The KHU
CHRISTED PURE BEING
Mystical Experience

The radical transformation of a person can occur after an authentic mystical experience where the Ba reflects back to the Ab and the Ab to the Khaibit. Then the mythic reality may be imploded and constructed with greater luminosity and clarity. The Khu, being so subtle, penetrates all lower bodies and exists temporarily in various states of consciousness and realms. Nirvana, Satori, and Cosmic Consciousness are some of the names of the Khu's interaction between the orders of Prime Source and a person's soul and bodies.

The Khu can perceive all the way through the quantum realm of subatomic particles into the Void, as well as read symbols; but unless it integrates the other bodies, there is danger that the person experiencing the Khu may go mad, or at best, construct a fragmentary view of reality. Knowledge of the divine realms is reserved for those who are Christed, and have integrated all nine bodies.

This means that he/she is humbly serving the good of the whole and speaks to people's deep unconscious or physical body even more than the personality or self-image.

Exercise

With all your body, heart and spirit, it is imperative with this exercise that you understand that it is all along the way to *becoming* unconditional love. It is not just that you be loving with someone, but that you open your heart and being to all beings everywhere. The characters in this book are moving in that direction, and yet it is not movement so much as stillpoint. Ceasing the quest is becoming one with the One. Surrendering to Prime Source is central for the Khu to be integrated. Such high spiritual integration is very rare, yet to intend that wholeness in an unconditional way is essential for true self-realization. Sometimes it occurs spontaneously.

1) Think of someone you used to hate or have resentment for, or perhaps still do. Go into your Ab (conscience) and ask for forgiveness for such feelings. Meditate deeply, being aware of your breath as it becomes more and more still as you go deeper. Accept any feelings you have that you'd like to be rid of, but witness yourself while doing so. Witness and feel. Witness and feel until you begin to feel happy, at peace, loving. This may take many hours, days, weeks, months, years. Be patient and unconditional and it will happen. Now send love to the person you previously had enmity for. If they are nearby and alive, do something for them, even if just inviting them over for lunch, or helping them with a project they are doing.

2) Create a regular time to go to the wilderness or walk in Nature. Even the city might be considered a wilderness, if you can just witness it and not interact during this exercise. If possible, walk everyday, or if not, then every week. Allow yourself to be nobody and nothing, knowing nothing and just open to the present moment. Empty yourself of all self-images, ideas of success, worries of family or anything else. Just let go of what you want, or what you're afraid of, and surrender to God. A vision quest with a fast (if done with an attendant who does not disturb, but simply provides water or juice) will also be a good context. Decide what limits (like fasting, not talking) you will impose on yourself. Such processes often meet with a lot of resistance from your ego or personality. Let your lower bodies have their say, but then go on towards deeper surrender, prayer, meditation of being in the stillpoint.

3) If you are facing some challenge or difficulty like terminal illness, or illness of any kind, a difficult spouse, or legal conflict, these can be good opportunities for releasing attachment to results. Bring your conscious awareness towards source rather than effect. Continue to practise this *Sourcing* all through the trial. Though you may lose what you feared, you will be closer to being one with your Khu.

Ariel

   has undergone many deep transformations of all twelve archetypes. She is still seeking to surrender her will to Prime Source, but has transmuted her anger and desires into greater care for those around her. As she ages, she grows wiser and more compassionate.

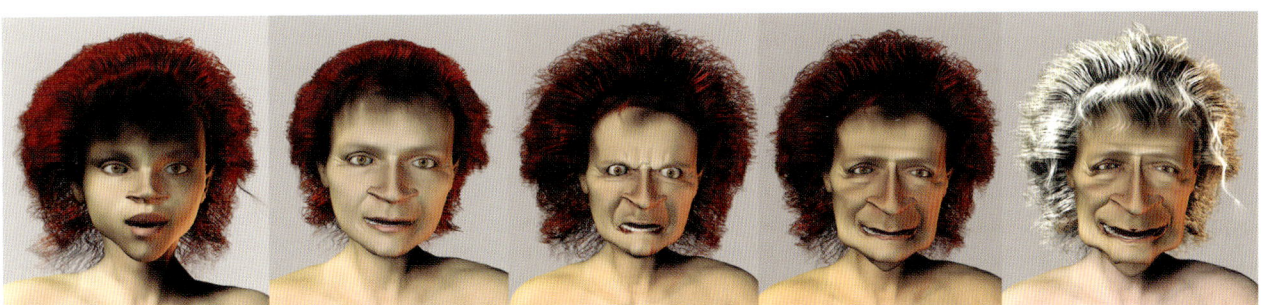

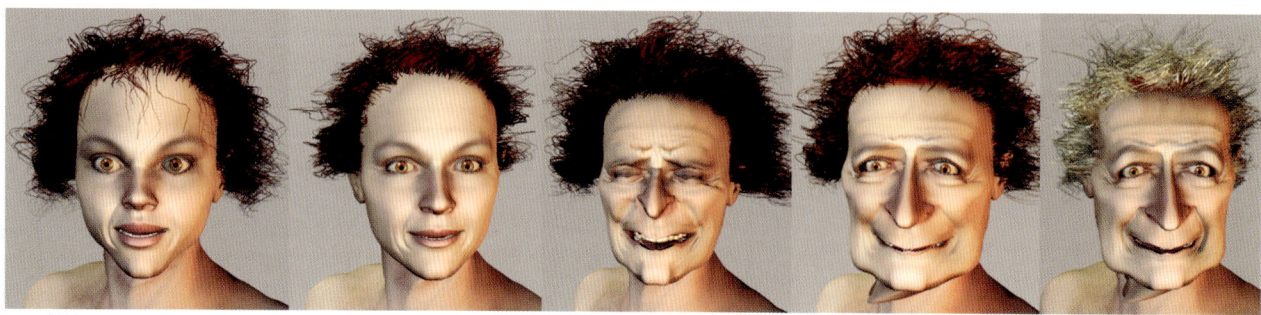

Shawn,

although a fighter, has grown more and more tender, open-hearted and is immune to what other people think unless their insights clarify his way to embodiment of love. He has become more and more unconditional in his approach to life and consequently is empathic and kind.

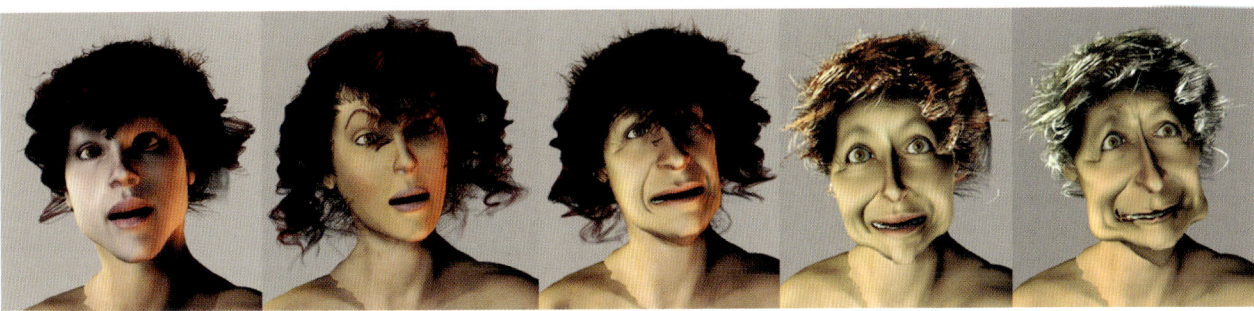

Elizabeth

has graced her life with more and more love. Her desires have begun to be sublimated (made sublime) and she is pointing in the direction of greater clarity. Her good heart enables her now to feel loved everywhere she goes.

Frank

doesn't fully understand himself, but he has transformed many frustrations into a steady, durable path of light. Although he is less reliable outwardly, he is deeply reliable within, for he is in touch with his Ab, which consistently tells him the truth.

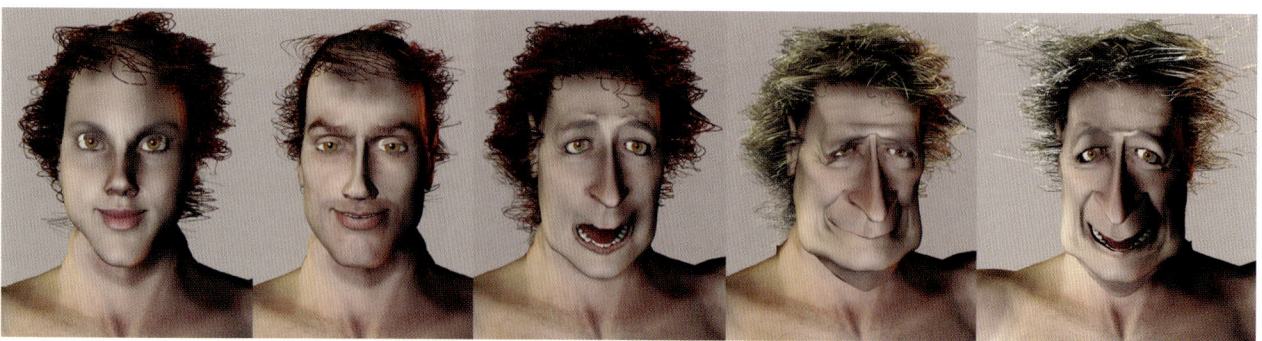

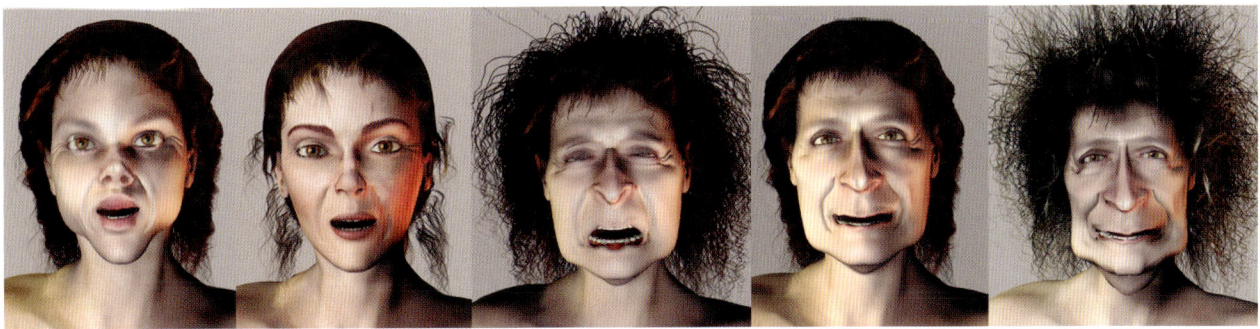

Karen

    is tolerant and wise, moving through life with fits and starts of paradoxical union with the One. She has had mystical experiences, which baffle her conscious mind and self-image, but she is more and more open to a sense of mystery. She is more willing to trust that there is a purpose to life.

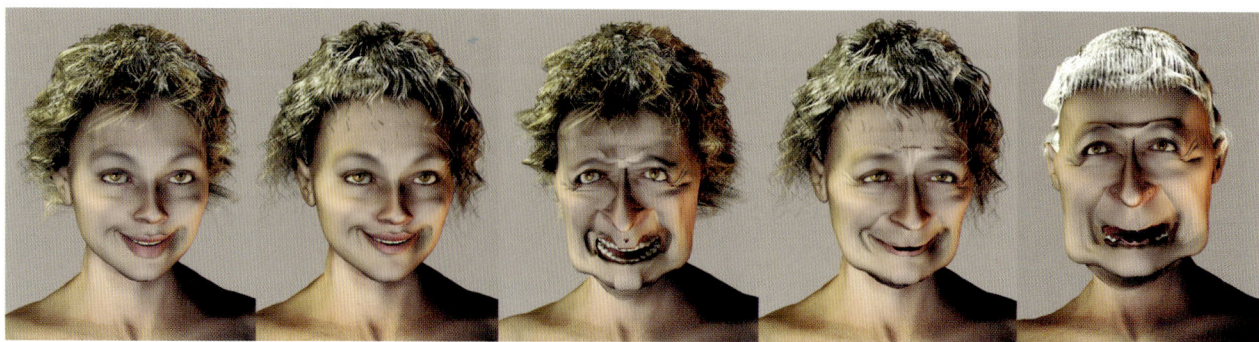

Morgan

has grown simpler in relation to the world, for his inventions support him in having the time to find supreme consciousness states. Still highly concentrated, he is now uniting his mind with his heart, opening to the great mysteries of the universe.

Jennifer

is living in somewhat of a stupor over direct experiences with eternal light. She is seeking to find ways to reconstruct her world view in accordance with the unknowable! Meanwhile, she is dancing with adults, the elderly, and children alike in public parks.

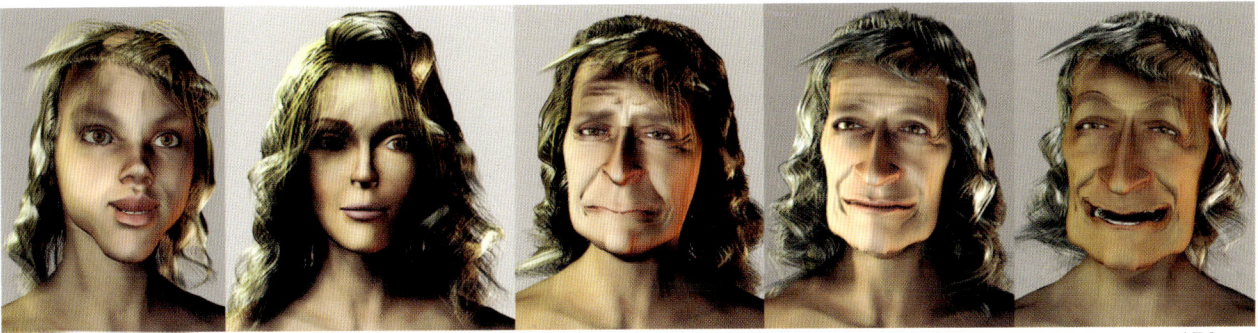

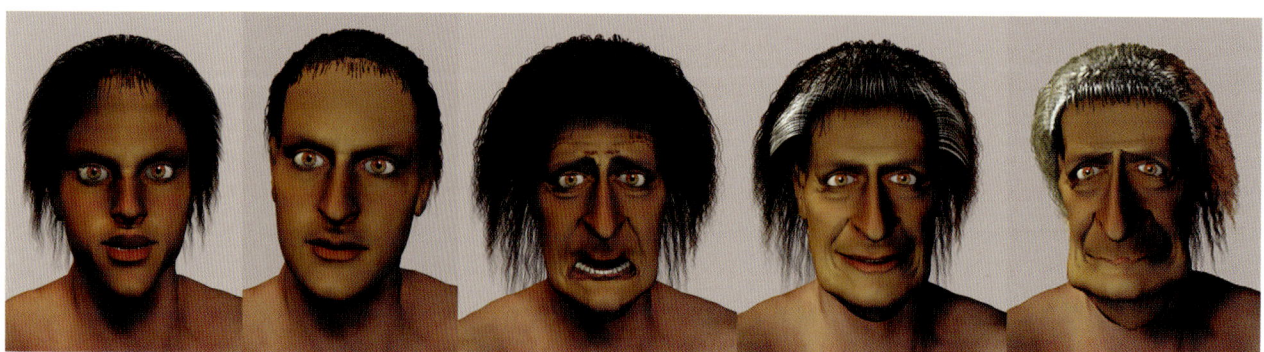

Ricardo

has a bright aura around him now, as he becomes more confident about his inner life. He has discovered, through numerous excursions, that the inner and outer worlds are not separate. He has released a need to control or be controlled and consequently is much happier.

Serafina's

     paintings reveal layers of light. She sees everything more transparently and as she sees, so her own aura becomes. She lives in ecstatic union with Nature, but is still finding deep communion with people somewhat challenging. Her Khu is penetrating all her other bodies when she responds through her art.

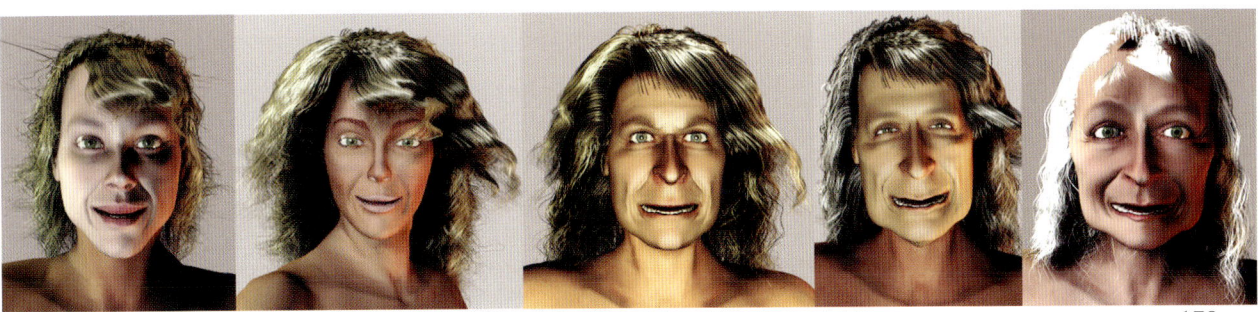

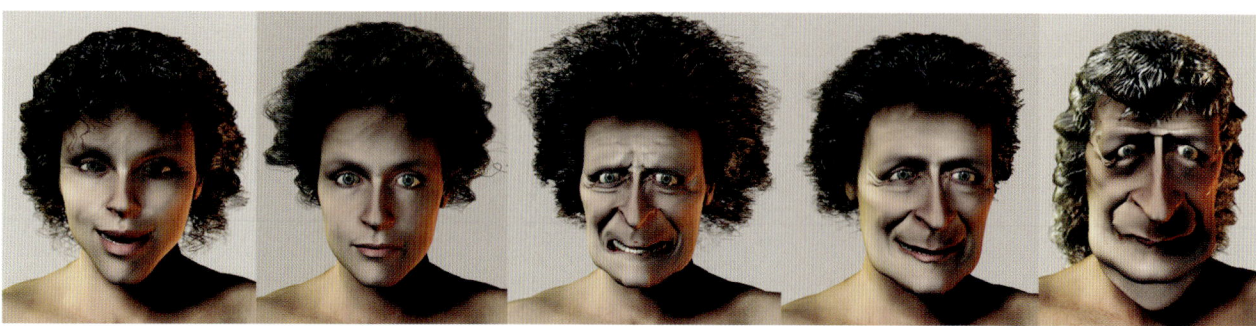

Francis

lives in the stillpoint almost continuously now, for he is surrendering more and more to the One. He prays and elevates his consciousness daily, so that the sublime experiences of heart-mind become more and more an inherent steady state.

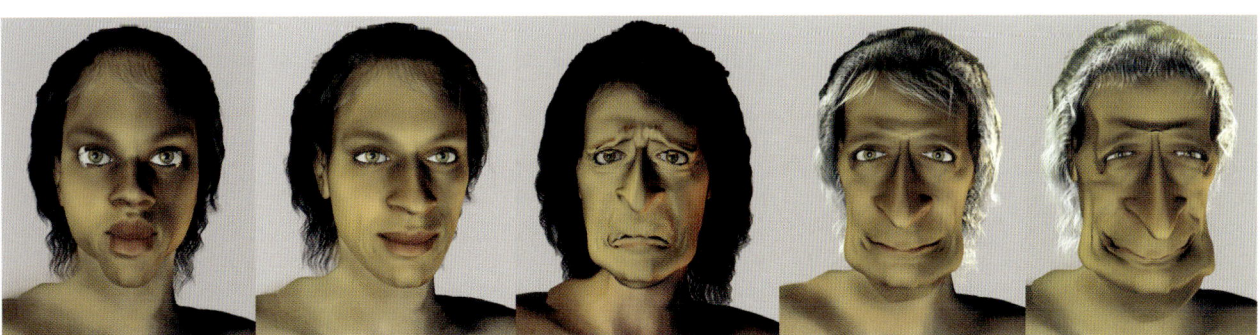

Francesca

has found more peace within herself, but is still struggling with self-acceptance on a deep level. Not acceptance of her personality, but acceptance that she is truly loved by God, the source of all. Her radiance is increasing and her heart more and more trusting, sometimes a painful process.

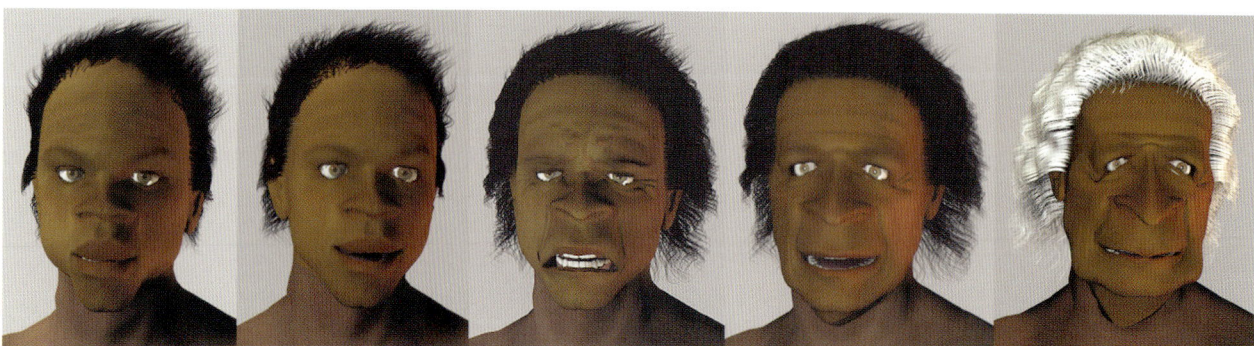

Ramon

has accepted that he might not be a famous filmmaker, but he is more sensitive and works with people in all walks of life. As a consequence, his films are actually better received by others. He reveals the One within each of his characters.

Dolores

has released most of her fears—of being a victim, of pain, of being unworthy—and she is opening to the subtle spheres of spiritual states. Her happiness comes from finding an equipoise in situations that previously would have thrown her off balance.

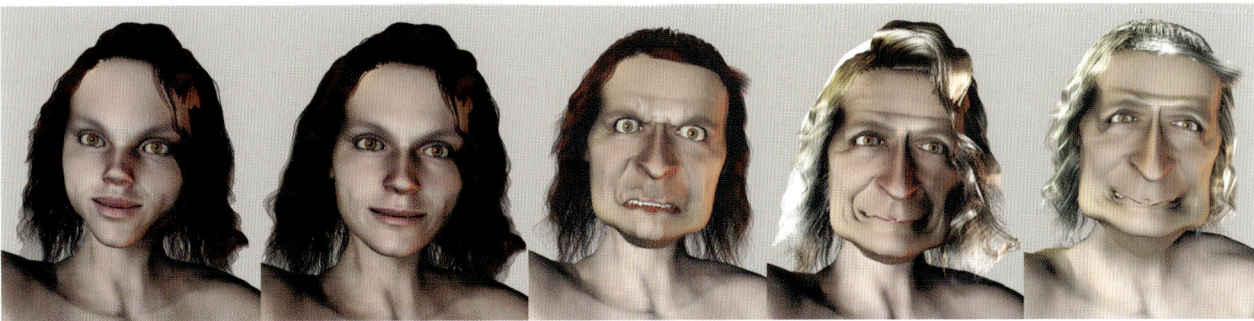

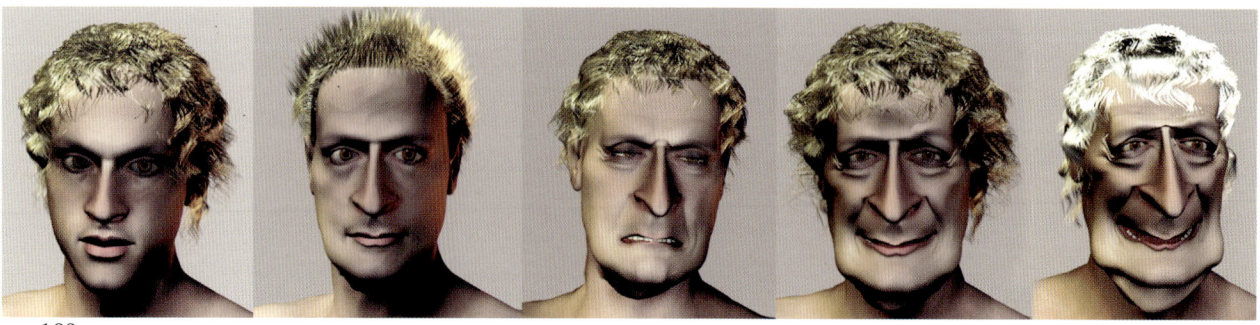

Horus

is more self-forgiving as he realizes that simple delights, like beholding the sky, petting a cat, or communing with his apparent "enemies," contain the supreme reality. In quiet moments, he reaches beyond the stars into dimensions that are unspeakable.

David

is singing to his heart's content, and through music he finds the intrinsic joy that carries him beyond his limited self. Although breaking through to pure being was difficult, it is more and more ordinary and familiar as he continues living in the present moment each day.

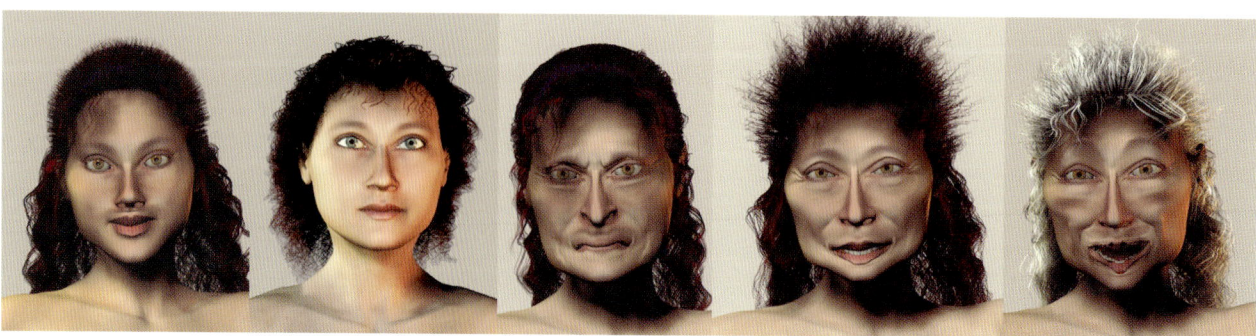

Ratta

is growing more refined as she tranmutes her sexual energy into ecstatic states of consciousness in relation to many different people. She is considered a wise woman among her community. Her own focus is on simply being humbly true to unconditional love in each NOW.

Humphrey

has become well-known for his articles and books, but now he doesn't care about that. His Khu often penetrates his other bodies, so then he moves through any fears and desires. Transformation of passion into compassion has become his central theme, in life and literature.

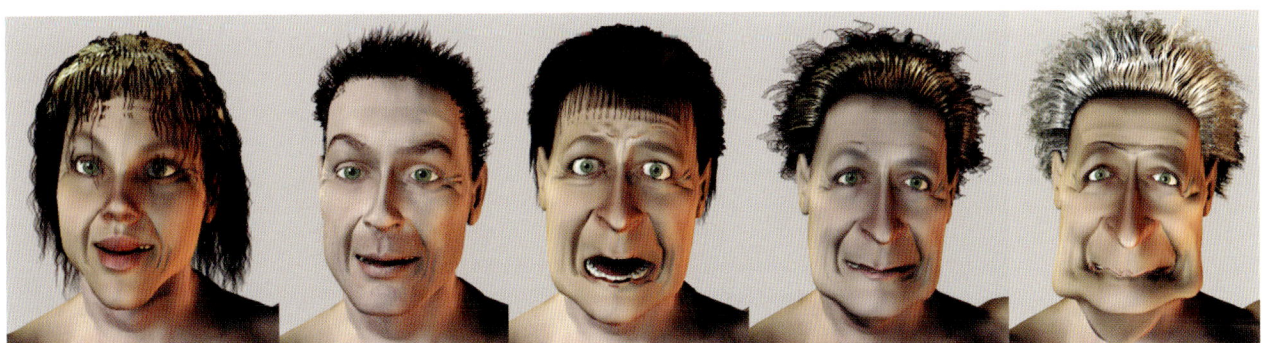

Clare

wears the robe of light that embodies all archetypes, but she is still primarily interested in transforming light codes. She works with students, in an initiatory way, even though there is no clear school. For her wisdom and love join in daily life.

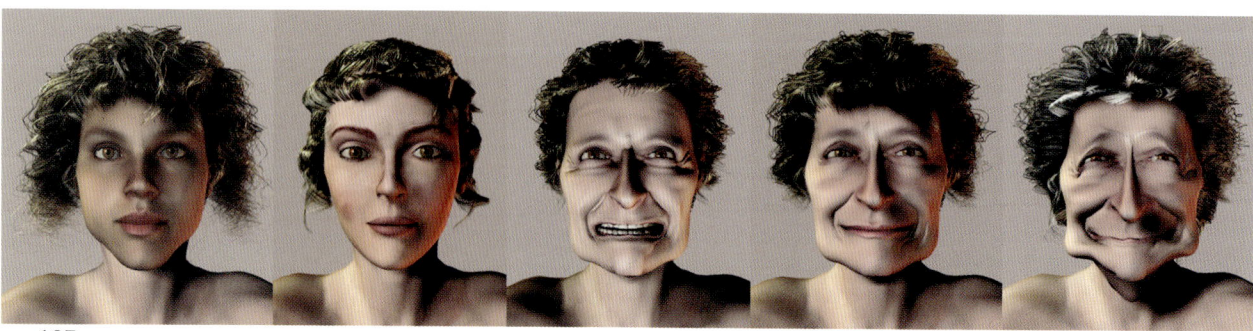

Shobak Shu's

love for Nature helps in surrendering to Source. He has journeyed far and wide, but knows that he is but a bubble in the great sea of life. He mediates heaven and earth, the invisible and visible worlds through staying calm and encouraging others with his deep love.

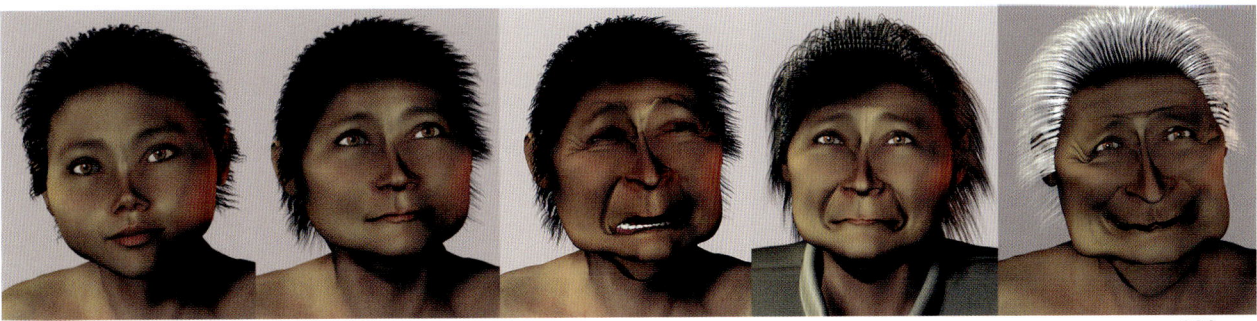

Janet

had a profound realization enabling her to see people with the same detachment she has for Nature. She is a compassionate witness to everything around her, and yet prays every night for Prime Source to send love to all suffering people.

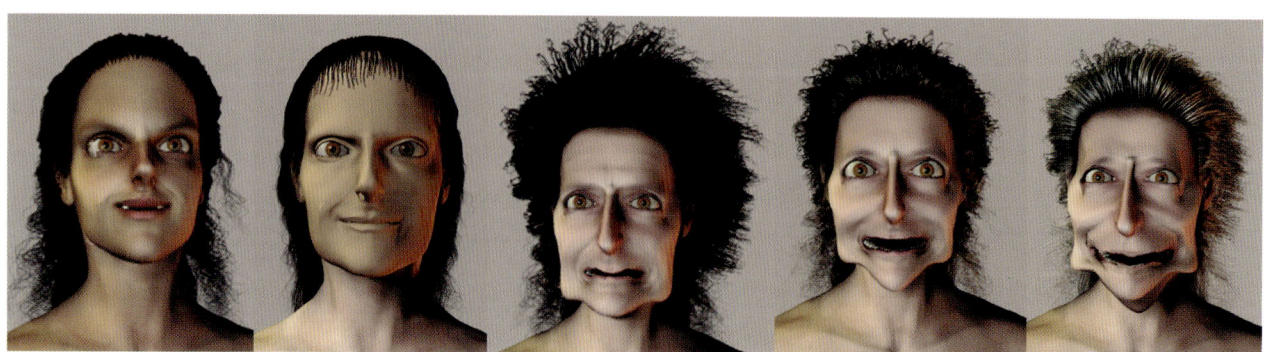

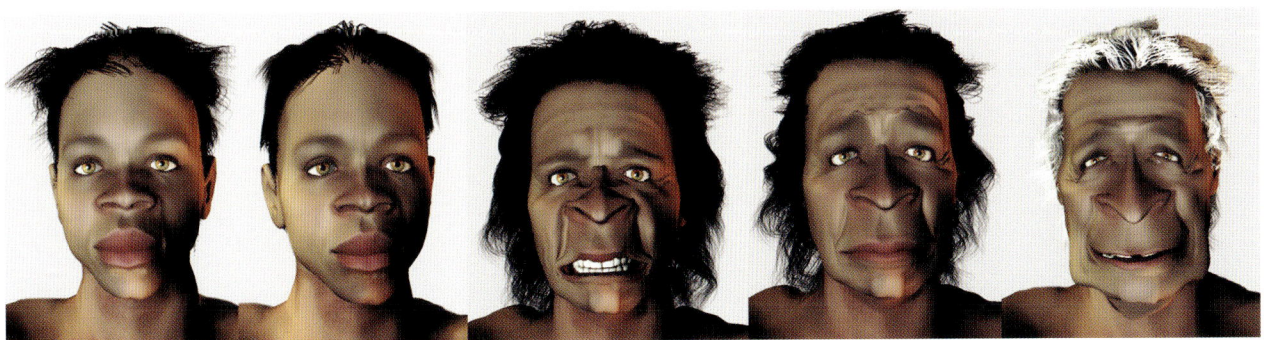

Joe

has undergone a profound death and rebirth that enables him to be more patient with others, as well as himself. He almost died from malaria on one of his trips, and this enables him to accept life as it comes. All the emotion tied up in anger before is now pure divine energy emanating from his being.

Wabadu

is still working for racial tolerance, but in a new way. She prays for goodness to come to all peoples, but has released all expectations. She keeps her feet on the ground, but is now very mellow and patient in her relationships. Every night she meditates until she comes into the stillpoint where peace resides.

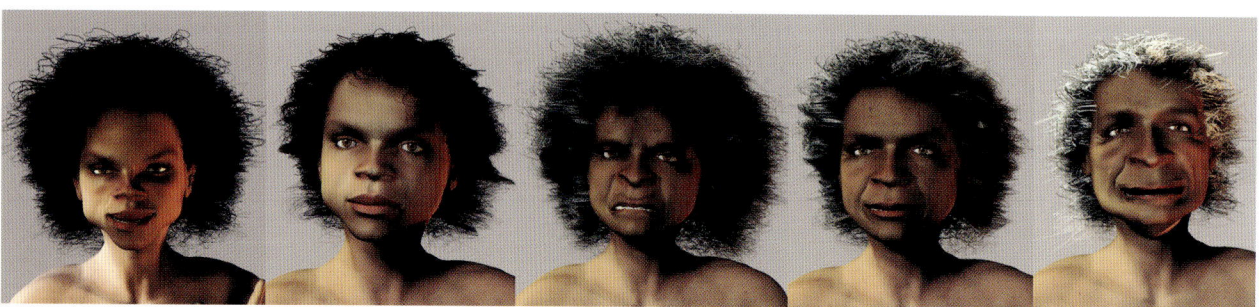

Ingalook

is learning more and more of the Way of Tao, and also of his Eskimo ancestors. He feels the sameness, the universal qualities in both. For him, it is living in the now, flexible, silent, and unpredictable as the wind. He surrenders to the Tao in every step of his life.

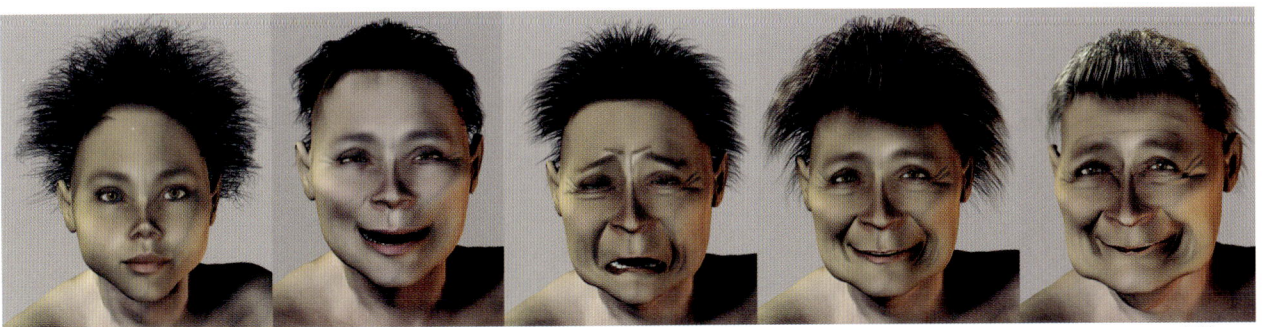

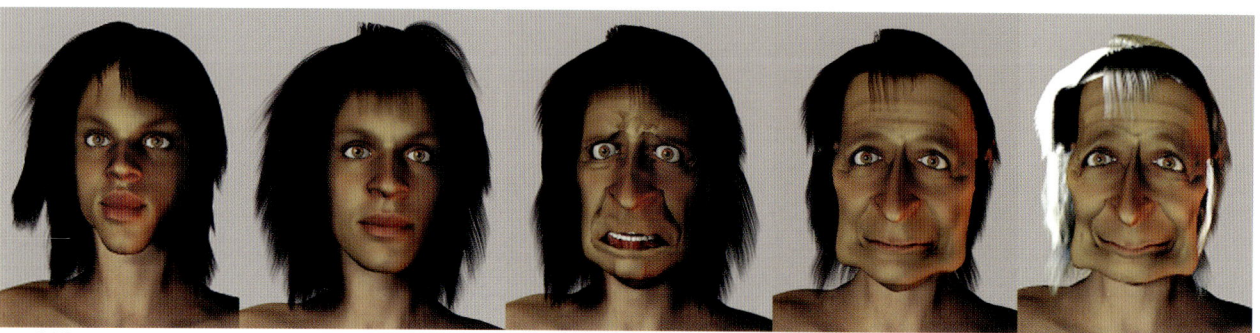

Radha's

    dark night of the soul forced her to become fearless. She walked through fear of humiliation, illness, death, and torture. So now her higher chakras are illuminated and her lower chakras are cleared for greater confidence. Now she is learning how to be in a loving state as continuously as possible.

May all beings be happy!

Other Works by Rowena Pattee Kryder

Books

Co-Creation Code Deck   isbn 0-9722747-0-7 $39.95

Sophia's Body: Seeing Primal Patterns in Nature   isbn 0-9624716-7-4 $35.95

Tiger and Dragon I Ching   isbn 0-9624716-6-6 $24.95

Source: Interpretations of Global Creation Myths   isbn 0-9624716-9-0 $16.95

Vibrational Healing Cards   isbn   0-9624716-5-8 $44

Sacred Ground to Sacred Space   isbn   1-879181-20-7 $24.95

Emerald River of Compassion   isbn   1-879181-13-4 $26.95

Destiny   isbn   0-9624716-8-2 $11

The Faces of the Moon Mother   isbn   0-9624716-2-3 $9

Gaia Matrix Oracle   isbn   0-9624716-1-5 $22

DVDs and VHS

Codes of Co-Creation (2 hour DVD)   isbn   0-9722747-2-3 $26

Codes of Co-Creation (2 hour VHS)   isbn   0-9722747-1-5 $30

Tree of Life and Art of the Tree of Life (VHS only) isbn 0-9624716-3-1 $34.95

Song to Thee: Divine Androgyne with Interspace and Passages (VHS only) $34.94

Audio

The Many Being One with the One (CD)   isbn   0-9722747-5-8 $15

Cosmic Voices (three casettes)   isbn 0-9624716-4-X $25

Posters

Sophia's Body—22" X 30" (four color) $15

Tiger and Dragon I Ching—4 black and white posters 19" X25" $20

www.creative-harmonics.org